HEAVEN'S WOMB

a theology of life and fruitfulness

"The Lord called me from the womb, from the body of my mother he named my name... he formed me from the womb to be his servant..."

Isaiah 49:1-5

"You are he who took me from the womb, you made me trust you at my mother's breasts. On you was I cast from my birth, and from my mother's womb you have been my God."

Psalm 22:9-10

HEAVEN'S WOMB

a theology of life and fruitfulness

by Susan Eby

Copyright © 2021 Susan O. Eby

All rights reserved. No part of this book may be reproduced or distributed in any form or by any means, or stood in a database or retrieval system—except for brief quotations in printed reviews—without prior written permission by the publisher.

Patria Media

Info@patriainstitute.com

Patria Media is a division of Patria Institute. The Institute's mission is to equip families to disciple their communities and their nation by means of a comprehensive Biblical worldview education. Patria Media accomplishes this through education and family publications.

Printed in the United States of America

ISBN 978-1-934856-07-9

Set in Google Font: Crimson & Crimson Pro

Cover Design by Joel Eby

Scripture quotations are from The Holy Bible English Standard Version, a publishing ministry of Good News Publishers. Used by permission. All right reserved.

Table of Contents

With Much Thanks

A sketch that arrived in my text messages depicted a stoic cat calmly sitting behind his desk concentrating on the manuscript in his hands. At the same time, sitting on the edge of his seat in front of the desk was an extremely eager dog, panting heavily while enthusiastically wagging his tail as he focused on his editor with great anticipation.

"Well first off," the cat is saying, "you tend to overuse the exclamation point."

I completely identified with the relevance of it when my friend Sarah Butler texted it to me, communicating editorial criticisms in her funny, gentle way. Sarah has been a true friend whose input and criticisms I gratefully welcome. She has consistently offered encouragement and suggestions every time I sat on the edge of my seat, panting and wagging my tail trying to communicate my exciting ideas to her. My heartfelt thanks go to her for the many times she has sacrificially read through what I have written.

My son, Joel Eby, is not so subtle as he tells me bluntly, "Mom, you *have* to stop using so many exclamation marks." Though far more straightforward than Sarah, I will always be eager and grateful for his expert criticisms, suggestions, and design work. I truly value his input. His skill far surpasses mine in every way imaginable, and not surprisingly, he's almost always right.

My daughter Sarah Rose has consistently given me encouragement to *write* as she's understood my heart more than almost anyone else.

Great appreciation goes to Cheryl Rogers who painstakingly combed through my manuscript, correcting it editorially and giving me such encouraging input regarding the content. One of life's greatest blessings is to call such women friends, who rejoice in the call of God on their lives, knowing they are created to reflect His Kingdom and live for His glory.

When I gave the manuscript to Pastor Michael Kloss ***(Redeemer Church, Lynnwood, WA)***, I would have been prepared to rewrite the whole book if he believed the theology was incorrect in any way. I trusted the soundness of his theology and his input that much. I'm very grateful for the time he carved out of his already full schedule as husband, father, pastor, and highly articulate theologian to give serious theological input and to so willingly write the Foreword.

Though I've never met her, Joni Eareckson Tada has inspired me with thoughts from her 1995 book Heaven, Your Real Home that sparked some of the ideas I've deeply pondered and expanded upon in this book. I look very much forward to many inspirational conversations with her in eternity, as well as with many who've already gone on– R.J.Rushdoony, G.K.Chesterton, C.S.Lewis, Peter, and the apostle Paul, to name a few.

It's impossible to even imagine my pursuit of God's Kingdom without the support and encouragement of a husband whose passion is likewise to glorify God in every part of life. I have great gratitude for my husband Dan Eby who shares my vision, feeds my enthusiasm, prays with me daily, reads everything I have ever written, and brings it all to fruition in the technical part of publishing a book. He's truly God's greatest gift to me.

And finally, I am deeply grateful for so many godly women in my life who have inspired the thoughts and ideas written in the following pages. I pray that every one of them will grasp the deep significance of how they were intentionally designed by God as living testaments that point to, and affirm the life and fruitfulness of the Kingdom of Heaven.

Foreword

In the wilderness of modern American evangelicalism, we need voices to call us to task, to call us to work and to call us to delight. Susan Eby arises among us as just such a voice; the delightful song of a fruitful matriarch, a garden well-tended by a faithful husband, faithful children and a faithful God. Susan writes, "While the world shamelessly parades a message of death and barrenness, in Christ Jesus we live triumphantly in the gospel message of life and fruitfulness." (p.10). Susan knows something of God's grace.

One quote we have discussed many times comes at the end of C.S. Lewis' essay, Is Theology Poetry: "I believe in Christianity as I believe that the Sun has risen, not only because I see it, but because by it I see everything else."1 And I can say that the sun of righteousness is always in her eyes, which means that when she speaks of what she sees, it is always saturated in Gospel. That is why her countenance is always bright. It is why laughter and song are often in her presence.

She is an adoring and devoted wife, demonstrating that beauty of disposition and character that can only come from a Christ-centered and loving marriage. I have experienced Eby hospitality; her son is my friend and fellow elder, and I have been delighted with stories about her from daughters-in-law and granddaughters. I've worshiped with her in the midst of

---

[1] Lewis, C.S. Weight of Glory (Collected Letters of C.S. Lewis. Harper Collins. Kindle Edition p.141

God's people. I have seen her engage in fellowship and feasts. She proves Psalm 16:11; "You make known to me the path of life; in your presence there is fullness of joy; at your right hand are pleasures forevermore."2 I have seen the joy and pleasure she takes in her husband, in her well-worn bible, in her three faithful children, in her eleven grandchildren, in friends and strangers, in laying a table and giving conference talks and singing in church. They are the joy and pleasure of one who stands firmly and securely at Christ's right hand.

In the book you hold, you will hear her laughter and song. Susan's joy and pleasure are the gospel, and she expresses a love for the things God loves, as a lady who knows her part and has been taught to follow the maestro faithfully. She offers a melodious tune, not an ivory tower philosophy or a pop-theology how-to guide. In the work that follows, you will see this joy.

But don't be fooled. As G.K Chesterton wrote, "The most extraordinary thing in the world is an ordinary man and an ordinary woman and their ordinary children." Susan knows that there is nothing more ordinary than a man and a woman and their womb. Nothing could be more common and lowly than a womb. And God descended into a womb to save the world. Susan knows that fruitfulness was commanded in the beginning (Genesis 1:28) and that marriage and the womb are the framework of redemptive history (John 3:3; Ephesians 5:32). Her wisdom is found in her sanctified delight in the

---

2 The Holy Bible: English Standard Version. (2016). Psalm 16.11. Wheaton, IL: Crossway Bibles,

things God delights in. The ordinary things. A living faith, in the living room.

Listen to her. Laugh with her. Cry with her. And with her, be enraptured by the ordinary.

Michael Kloss
Pastor, Redeemer Church, Lynnwood, Washington
February 2021

Introduction

"Dear friends," the email began, "thank all of you for the kind words, prayers, and patience as Peter and I decided how to move forward with our wedding. Due to our state's stay-at-home extension, Peter and I have decided to cancel our wedding as previously planned..."

...and my heart simply broke for this young bride. Like so many others, she had dreamed of her special day since she was a little girl, only to have her dreams completely shattered on the very brink of their fulfillment by a strangely anticipated pandemic that somehow succeeded to shut down the entire world, cripple the livelihood of millions, and cause utter chaos, frustration– and, yes, broken dreams.

Life as we have always known it remains at a standstill after more than a year. It was all so sudden, not gradual as we would have expected this kind of thing to be. It never gave us enough time to think about creative ideas for "Plan B" weddings, or to find alternative ways of making a living when our businesses were shut down, or to withhold having children until the world was safe enough for our kids to inherit it– or at the very least, to make sure we had enough supplies to last us as long as the lockdown would demand.

This kind of thing has never happened before in the history of the world, and whether or not we will ever find out the real facts of what brought this about, it's clear that stopping the whole world was a relatively easy– and fast– thing to do.

Each morning, I wake wondering incredulously how it is that every normal aspect of life has so suddenly become *ab*normal. My husband and I sat at our breakfast table and the absurdity of our conversation – about how we could actually be arrested for simply opening up our business or for going to church– left me completely incredulous. Will life ever be normal, I wonder? What lessons will we have learned from this? What will our priorities be from now on? And for goodness sake, what are we supposed to be *doing* during this strange and abnormal time?

Trying to figure out how to live life within the crux of our confinement to house arrest was certainly challenging, and that's how we will forever remember that it was. Added to that, trying to grasp the reality of our faith in the midst of it has also been a test of gigantic proportion. Will there *ever* be conversation outside of "the pandemic" again?

Writing a book is a long, hard task, and I had been working on this book long and hard when the lockdown was inflicted upon us. In a mere moment, the content of it suddenly seemed so insignificant. Irrelevant. Unimportant. The idea of God's Kingdom being characterized by "life and fruitfulness" seemed disconnected– so bland in the greater context of this world crisis.

Until I got the email mentioned above.

In truth, I'd found myself dragging my feet each day with a despondency as though this was the end of life as we've known it. With our liberties snatched away and anti-Christian influences so blatantly invading our world, I'd erroneously resigned myself to subconsciously assuming that we are all now subjected to merely marking time until we get to heaven and find our freedom in Christ once again. I had found myself living under a foggy cloud of resignation to the successful coercion of "the enemy," I guess.

Until that email rattled me awake. And just as suddenly and powerfully as the lockdown news had hit us, Jeremiah 29 came shouting– or "dancing," perhaps– into my mind.

This chapter of the Bible tells of the letter Jeremiah sent to the Israelites who had been taken from Jerusalem into captivity in Babylon. Specifically, it gave them instructions about how they were to live life while under the restraints of being prisoners in exile, in captivity:

> "Thus says the Lord of hosts, the God of Israel to all the exiles...Build houses and live in them; plant gardens and eat their produce. Take wives and have sons and daughters; take wives for your sons, and give your daughters in marriage, that they may bear sons and daughters; multiply there, and do not decrease. But seek the welfare of the city where I have sent you into exile, and pray to the Lord on its behalf, for in its welfare you will find your welfare..." (Jeremiah 29:4-7)

God has called us to live above our circumstances. He has given us very significant tasks to accomplish *while* we are in captivity: get married; have children; increase; and change the place of our captivity into one that glorifies God so that we ourselves might be healthy in every respect– in our spirits, our minds, our bodies.

The dominion mandate that God gave to man in Genesis 1:28 to "be fruitful and multiply, replenish the earth and subdue it" was not given to the exclusion of a virus or the illegitimate edicts of elected officials who are enjoying the tight grip they're holding on us. The dominion mandate was given to man for always, *even* in captivity.

The brides whose plans have been overturned have had to make some huge adjustments amid big disappointments. But even within that context, they are glorifying God by *getting married.*

Parents need not fear raising their children during very difficult times of captivity. They are a significant part of God's answer! Raising the next generation of Godly children is our response to His command to overturn adverse times: *increase* and raise faithful children for the glory of God. Planting gardens, building houses, seeking the welfare of the place where we live are all acts of obedience to the commands of God in order to take dominion and overcome the enemy.

If we've ever needed to be reminded of the message of "life and fruitfulness" that God has given to those of us who live in His Kingdom, it's *now.* God's Word to us has not changed. Our circumstances may have changed, but His command to us has not. The Kingdom of God is characterized by life and fruitfulness and nothing that happens around us will ever change that.

God commands us to increase, not decrease. Now is not the time for us to pull back or mark time. It's a time to increase, to move forward, to live life to the fullest.

Ours is a message of hope, of life, of increase. No enemy can ever take that from us.

Plans may change, but brides will keep on getting married; gardens will keep on being planted; houses will still get built; babies will keep on being born; life will keep going on– because no enemy can ever defeat the life and fruitfulness that characterizes the very heart of the Kingdom of God to which we belong.

God's message of life and fruitfulness does not become irrelevant in the face of a lockdown or even a socialist takeover. On the contrary- it's the very weapon with which we will conquer the enemy.

CHAPTER 1
In Him We Live

Time is a strange and peculiar character that we have no choice but to live with. For the most part, I admit that I enjoy a relatively peaceful coexistence with time. I do my part, and time does his. I make appointments, and time makes sure I keep them.

Time even gives me considerable help when I need to arrange a way to be with family or friends, and generally makes it possible to keep a fairly comfortable rhythm and necessary order in my life.

But every once in awhile, time behaves like a stubborn scoundrel, refusing to accommodate the legitimate need for it to slow down, or maybe even stop altogether once in awhile, just long enough for us to catch our breath and to process certain events– good ones as well as bad ones; birth as well as death. But it doesn't. It won't. Time flatly refuses to adjust to anything other than its own determined speed.

No matter how much I might beg for it to slow down, time– that rogue fourth dimension– keeps pushing relentlessly onward, forcing us into submission to its own unyielding persistence. Our kids grow swiftly into parents themselves, and with lightning speed, grandchildren grow into adults as we're swept along by the constant flow of time, breathlessly trying to keep up with it all. Time forces us into the future, even as it so harshly separates us from our past.

Fifteen years have flown by since my dad died, and yet I still haven't successfully grasped how it is that time has pushed us ahead that fast. After fifteen long years, certain triggers still bring the sound of his voice into my head with such clarity that it feels like I'd heard him just last week– a particular laugh, an old song, certain scriptures. Acutely aware of his own weaknesses and shortcomings, my dad found his hope and strength in the Bible, so he prayed Scripture; he sang Scripture; he exhorted us with Scripture– not because he was attempting to convince us of his own righteousness, but in true humility he wanted to constantly point us to the great hope in the finished work of Christ alone for those of us who fail. And I could identify with that.

After all this time– fifteen long years– it's my dad's voice I still hear almost audibly when I read Acts 17:28, "In Him we live and move and have our being." I'd heard him say it *so* many times.

In Him. How I wish I could tell my dad how much those simple little words have become such a rock of stability to me. But I can't, because time has carried him away into a place that I don't have access to right now, even though it's very close, as you will read about in the pages ahead. My father captured my attention with those simple yet profound words, but it was through motherhood that their reality came so alive to me.

> "If anyone is **in Christ**, he is a new creation," it says in 2 Corinthians 5:17
>
> "...we are complete **in Him**," says Colossians 2:10

> "There is no condemnation for those who are **in Christ Jesus**," Romans 8:1
>
> "... **in Him** we become the righteousness of God," 2 Corinthians 5:21
>
> "**In him** we live, and move, and have our being... " Acts 17:28

It shouldn't come as a surprise that an ever-increasing understanding of what it means to be **in Him** has become clearer to me because of who I am as a woman, a wife, and especially a mother. Though time has swallowed up an incredible number of years since I carried children, it's impossible to forget what it was like– or the startling similarities in the way that a baby growing in utero shows us how it is that we grow in Christ. In the truest sense of the word, it's awesome that God designed such distinct roles for men and women in such a way that we can understand more about **who He is** by embracing **who we are,** designed uniquely by Him for procreation– for life and fruitfulness.

The idea of being this secure in my womanhood is a peaceful oasis in our turbulent culture that seems so confused over something as basic as gender. As silly as this seemed just a short time ago, right now there are those who honestly believe that the only way to calm the frustrating restlessness that constantly agitates them is to create a whole new identity by getting rid of the distinct differences between the sexes, trying to confuse male/female roles and compete **against** each other for equal achievement. But refusing to embrace the male/female distinction He created us with is to defy God's mandate for us–the very purpose for which we were created exactly as He made us.

The strangely deceptive idea in this current chapter of history, even among Christian evangelicals, is that this pursuit of "coloring outside of the lines" is progressive– even an attractive attribute. Yet in a lecture a generation ago, British journalist and theologian G.K. Chesterton addressed the deception so well:

> "I say we must have definite lines; but it is not because definite lines are the things which restrain humanity. [It's] because definite lines are what distinguish humanity. Our black lines are not the bars of the tiger's cage. They are the stripes of the tiger's skin: they are what makes him a tiger."[3]

God Himself, by His design, has created the black lines of humanity. At the very beginning, God created male and female and commissioned them to work together as one complete unit. His purpose was that together male and female would

> "be fruitful and multiply and fill the earth and subdue it, and have dominion over...every living thing that moves on the earth," (Genesis 1:28).

His divine mandate for His creation reflects the very character and nature of His Kingdom as being that of life and fruitfulness.

---

[3] Dale Ahlquist, *Common Sense 101 Lessons from G.K. Chesterton, (San Francisco, Ignatius Press, 2006), 21*

We shouldn't be surprised to find that running away from who God created us to be won't bring peace. And certainly, attaining equal achievement between the sexes won't bring peace. Trying to change yourself or trying to change others will never bring peace. (Admit it, you've tried.)

That nagging restlessness will never be settled by trying to create an identity for ourselves apart from God's design, but by finding our identity **in Him**– in the God who made us and designed us with precision and purpose. Paul wrote in Philippians 3:8,9 that he frankly counted all of his own achievements as mere rubbish, "that I may gain Christ and be found **in Him.**"

Peace can never be found in man, but by **being found in God**.

As humans, we're deceived if we think that this life is all about us and whatever it takes to make us happy. It isn't. Even as Christians, we're deceived if we think that salvation is merely for our own everlasting happiness. It isn't. We have a far better and much higher purpose that extends far beyond us. It's all God's Story, and He designed us intentionally for the purpose of revealing the life and fruitfulness of His Kingdom. He has created us to participate in **His** Story. This particular time in history may seem very uncomfortable to us, but we were intentionally created for this time–right now– for the sake of **His** Story. What a privilege!

Life is so much more than just us. God is the ultimate joy, and we will never find lasting satisfaction apart from Him.

Augustine famously said, "Thou has formed us for Thyself, and our hearts are restless till they find rest **in Thee.**"[4]

We have so much unlearning to do. The marks of the world run deep, even in Christians. In so many ways, we've been duped, brainwashed into thinking like the world does far too often. Somehow, we obsess over "our identity" just like the world does. We cater to that relentless craving to achieve success for ourselves as man defines it.

As women, we compete against men instead of completing them as God has designed us to. We're embarrassed when others find out that we're "just a mom." We've been deceived into agreeing that children are a burden, a hardship, or at the very least, a distraction from what's *really* important– like having a career, or having the freedom to travel, or accumulating enough money to get the things we really want. Even as this is being written, the actress Michelle Williams has made headlines for holding up her Golden Globe as she gushed that this coveted golden image would not have been possible had she not murdered her child by way of abortion.

But we've got it so wrong when we strive to reach outside of God's design, grasping at the illusive "other" in the futile attempt to find ourselves.

Author Dale Ahlquist perceptively noted how ludicrous it is for women to constantly grasp for satisfaction outside of their God-created design when he wrote that,

---

[4] Augustine, *Enarrationes in Psalmos 127.9.*

> "feminists claim they want the woman to have more influence in society, and then [ironically] they take her away from the place where she has the greatest of all influence in society: the home. They exalt public life: glitter and fuss and an emphasis on all the things that are false. Public life is fragmented, narrow, and temporary. Private life– that is, family life– is full and universal and is even a reflection of eternity."[5]

G.K. Chesterton wrote,

> "The place where babies are born, where men die, where the daily drama of mortal life is acted is not an office or shop or a bureau. It is something much smaller in size, yet much larger in scope. And while nobody would be such a fool as to pretend that the home is the only place where people should work, or even the only place where women should work, it has a character of unity and universality that is not found in any of the fragmentary experiences of the office or the shop or the bureau."[6]

Chesterton understood the vital impact of a godly woman, with her husband, shaping the lives of their children for the glory of God and the advancement of His Kingdom on the earth.

Our faith paints a completely different picture of fulfillment and purpose than the world does. Psalm 128 adds color and

---

[5] Dale Ahlquist, *Common Sense 101- Lessons from G.K Chesterton, (San Francisco, Ignasius Press, 2006), 147.*
[6] Ibid, 148

depth to our Christian faith as we find our identity in God and fulfill the purpose for which we were created, male and female:

> "...Your wife will be like a fruitful vine within your house; your children will be like olive shoots around your table. Thus shall the man be blessed who fears the Lord."

God's highest blessing to man is fruitfulness.

Children are God's blessing, and raising godly children is the most powerful way that we are called to conquer the enemy around us. Children are a good thing– a *very* good thing. In fact, it's through children– and motherhood and fatherhood– that we can so clearly understand God and His Kingdom. In Matthew 19:14 Jesus embraced the little ones and said,

> "Let the little children come to me and do not hinder them, for to such belongs the kingdom of heaven."

If Jesus emphasized the high value of having children, then our own perception of raising children really ought to change to be like His.

If we can really grasp it, there is probably nothing in the world that can give us such a clear picture of the life and fruitfulness that characterizes what it means to be found **in God** as clearly as a child growing in his mother's womb. The privilege that we women have of participating in such a breathtaking reflection of Almighty God as He designed us to be is so far beyond anything we'd imagined, and more powerful a weapon against the enemy than we can ever know.

Nothing can draw us closer to Him than to embrace the way He designed us. When we not only accept it, but delve deeply into the masterful way in which God designed the individual from conception, we will be awed and inspired to realize that the process of a man and a woman creating new life, and the child that grows out of their love, is an intentional reflection of our spiritual life in the Kingdom of God.

As active participants in the family of God, we ought to be ignited with passion about being born into the Kingdom of Heaven as we see it revealed so beautifully through life's greatest miracle, children being born into the world, brought into being through the unity of a man and a woman. What a great privilege God has given us– male and female– to share in this miracle and so reflect the greatest of kingdoms, that of Heaven.

There's no question that time is a relentless force that constantly pushes us out of our comfort zone, and yet there are some things that time can never change–like this age old reality. God's truth stands forever. While the world shamelessly parades a message of death and barrenness, **in Christ Jesus** we live triumphantly in the Gospel message of life and fruitfulness.

Like the child resting in the comfort, peace, and security of his mother's womb, we can know comfort, peace, and security as we rest in Him. So let's take a closer look, and be amazed as we consider the perfect design of God when He created man and woman and gave to them the joy of participation in the miracle of conception and birth– the perfect picture of our new birth into the Kingdom of God.

Acts 17:28 says that:

> "In Him we live, and move, and have our being– because we are indeed his offspring."

CHAPTER 2

New Life–What an Experience!

The day I gave birth to my first child, time stood still.

Well, it didn't really, of course. But it *felt* like it did. Maybe it *should* have.

Every mother knows the feeling, no matter what her circumstances are. After giving birth, a mother just can't seem to grasp the inconsistency of why life is continuing to go on around her as though nothing miraculous had just happened. Why didn't the world stop to reverently acknowledge a miracle?

Birth, like death, feels as though time is standing still– or *should* stand still. The awe and sacredness of both birth and death are the only experiences we know that bring us to the very edge of eternity where time is not as we know it. It's in those sacred moments that earth touches heaven. Time touches timelessness. Mortal man touches the miraculous.

And yet the miracle of birth can't be merely described in order to be fully comprehended. You have to know it. It has to be grasped– *experienced*– in order to truly comprehend it.

Once, on a foolish whim, I asked my husband, "Aren't you disappointed that you'll never know what it's like to give birth?" A baffled look spread over his face, wondering why I would even ask. He stared at me for a few seconds, then shrugged as he responded with what seemed obvious. "No."

What else should I have expected? After having stayed right by my side as he witnessed the suffering and pain of my labor, that was all he could perceive. And no person in his right mind would be attracted to pain and suffering.

Because he had never personally experienced childbirth, it will never be possible for him to grasp the incomprehensible degree of exhilaration that I had experienced at that moment of giving birth, a euphoria that made all the pain and labor worthwhile. As an onlooker–even a very close one– he had witnessed the great degree of cost I had paid, but he could never know the great degree of elation.

> "When a woman is giving birth, she has sorrow because her hour has come, but when she has delivered the baby, she no longer remembers the anguish for joy that a human being has been born into the world," Jesus told His disciples in John 16:21.

Such elation can only be grasped through something that's truly extraordinary– and childbirth *is* extraordinary. The mother has just participated in a miracle of bringing *life* into the world. There is nothing else like it, and the incredible exhilaration cannot be fully comprehended unless it's been experienced first hand. My husband's immediate recollection of birth as an observer is pain and labor; my immediate recollection, experientially, is the indescribable joy.

It's mind-boggling to me that the details of one single day that happened decades ago can still be etched so vividly in my memory after all this time– the day I gave birth to my first child. And honestly, memories of my other children's births are still just as clear, every one, and no less miraculous because miracles can never become tiresome when you recognize that they are miracles. Author Dale Ahlquist quoted Chesterton as saying that every time a baby is born, it's as if a whole new world has been created, seen for the first time by a new soul as if it were the first day of creation. [7]

Every mother knows that giving birth is something truly extraordinary, though circumstances certainly vary. Gratefully, all of my birth experiences, though painful, were fast, uncomplicated, and culminated in tremendous joy. For me, those actual moments of birth always came as an unexpected surprise, as though I should have been laboring far longer in order to reap the intense joy of such a trophy.

"He's so beautiful!" I literally cried at the first glimpse of my funny-looking, tiny, wrinkled, scowling, messy, squalling firstborn baby boy. "It's a miracle! It's a miracle!" I kept repeating, until the laughing nurse assisting my doctor remarked, "Yes, it *is* a miracle! And this isn't even church."

When the infant boy was laid in my arms, I couldn't stop staring at him with incomprehensible wonder at seeing such a tiny, living reflection of myself. My husband and I had just replicated a human being that had clear features of *us*.

---

[7] Dale Ahlquist, *Common Sense 101: Lessons from G.K.Chesterton, (San Francisco, Ignatius Press 2006), 31*

Our baby was completely helpless, unable to do anything to earn my affection, yet I had never known such intense love as I had for him. The baby I held in my arms was unable to communicate, was weak, hungry, confused– yet I knew without a doubt that I would give my life for his. From that moment on, my life was never the same.

Sleep alluded me all night long, as a simple yet profound song played itself over and over and over in my head: "Praise You, Father; Bless You, Jesus; Holy Spirit, thank You for being here, being near..."

Birth– like all the best parts of life– points to God. Spiritual birth is not just a coincidental reflection of natural childbirth. No, it's completely the other way around! Birth into the Kingdom of God is the true reality, and natural childbirth is a sacred reflection, an intentional design that points us to the true reality.

This was a reminder that C.S.Lewis wrote about:

> "I must take care, on the one hand, never to despise or be unthankful for these earthly blessings, and on the other hand, never to mistake them for the something else of which they are only a kind of copy, or echo, or mirage." [8]

Unfortunately, there *are* mothers who do despise their childbirth experiences. There are some who are unthankful,

---

[8] C.S. Lewis, *Mere Christianity, (San Francisco, Harper Collins Edition, 2001), 137*

unable to recognize that every child is a gift, a living soul created in the image of God. Blinded by pain or by sin– their sin, or someone else's– they are unable to comprehend the great privilege we have been given to reflect the eternal.

On the other hand, there are also mothers who worship their children, as though their children were the reality, not the copy that points to the reality. In The Great Divorce, Lewis wrote of the painful experience of the mother who would have chosen rather to be in hell with her son than to be separated from him in heaven. [9]

Lewis was wise to identify the source of discontent and ingratitude for what it is. As he warned us, we must be cautious to never despise nor be unthankful for this great blessing that God gives, and yet at the same time, never regard it as the true reality but the reflection, the echo of the true reality.

Probably the greatest pitfall of mankind is a perpetual temptation to either despise what God has created, or to worship and serve it– the creature– instead of the Creator (Romans 1:25); to become so focused on man, one way or the other, that we don't see God.

With that in mind, let's consider the true reality– how Jesus knew this elation in a greater way than any of us can or will ever know. Whenever we think of the sacrifice that Jesus bore through his crucifixion, we tend, rightfully, to focus on the

---

[9] C.S.Lewis, *The Great Divorce, (New York, NY, McMillan Publishing, 1974) Chapter 11*

unfathomable pain He suffered in order to deliver us out of the darkness of sin that enveloped every one of us. We didn't have to bear that great burden of pain, though the sin was rightfully ours. By God's grace, we were only observers. As onlookers, we see the great pain and the great cost He bore.

And yet at the end of His suffering, there was incomprehensible elation that only Jesus Himself has experienced after He had fully obeyed the Father, submitted to such unimaginable suffering, and paid the full price so that through faith in Him, *we* who were weak, hungry, confused, helpless could be born into His everlasting Kingdom. More than observers, *we* were the ones who were born through His suffering. And as we share in His suffering, we share in His joy (2 Timothy 2:12).

> Psalm 127:3 says, "Behold, children are a heritage from the Lord, the fruit of the womb a reward."

The infant child is the *reward* of a mother's pain and intense labor, just as we who are brought into the Kingdom of Heaven are the reward of Jesus' pain and suffering. *We* are the reward of His suffering– not the pure, the brilliant, the beautiful, the talented– but the weak, the confused, the helpless, the hungry.

Imagine that moment when Jesus cried out, "It is finished!" These words were not a resignation of defeat, but a bold declaration of *victory!* What incomprehensible joy–*elation*– Jesus must have experienced at that precise moment, when He had fully accomplished the perfect will of His Father. Jesus' perfect obedience to the Father through suffering was complete. Finished.

> "...Looking to Jesus, the founder and perfecter of our faith who for the joy that was set before him, endured the cross, despising the shame, and is seated at the right hand of the throne of God," (Hebrews 12:1,2).

Job is one of our earliest records of one who experienced new birth at the end of his intense suffering and trials. Clearly, from the beginning of Job's life, God had elected him and chosen him. "Have you considered my servant Job," God said to Satan, "...blameless and upright?" Job was a righteous man in all his works, yet when he was finally worn down to his lowest point– weak, depressed, confused– Job recognized that up until this experience of encountering the living God through his suffering:

> "I had heard of you by the hearing of the ear, but now my eye sees you; therefore I despise myself and repent in dust and ashes..." (Job 42:5,6).

There's *hearing* about Him, and then there's truly *seeing* Him, *grasping* Him. And when we truly see God, we also see ourselves for who we really are– sinners whose own righteousness is nothing more than filthy rags (Romans 3:10.) We can only know God when like Job, we have experienced Him first hand. Having truly known the forgiveness of our sins through His suffering, and having our eyes opened to faith in Him, we can never be the same.

Right now in our culture there's a plethora of theists- those who have heard about Him and agree that God (or gods) exists in some form. And then there are true "believers," those who have *seen* Him and unquestionably believe that Jesus Christ is the Son of the one true God, that He suffered for us in order to pay the penalty of our miserable weakness and sin, that we might be born into abundant life.

Our new birth must be experienced firsthand in order to truly grasp it. There is no other way. We might think we understand what "new birth" is from hearing what others say about it, from explanations, sermons, and descriptions. We might think we know what it is because we can repeat the right words and terminology, or because we can quote all the right scriptures about it.

We might even think we know what it is because as very close observers, we've witnessed others around us being born again. But observers–even close ones– only see the cost, the pain. They cannot fully comprehend the joy of rebirth until they've experienced it for themselves.

Like the difference between a beautiful painting and the true reality of the landscape that the painting represents, childbirth is an intentionally designed copy that points us to our true birth into the everlasting Kingdom of Heaven. As wonderful as it is, natural childbirth is a divine **reflection** that helps us to understand the miraculous reality of birth into the Kingdom of Heaven.

What joy our Father God must have when we become more and more like Him, growing in Him until the day when we will see Him face to face. What elation there must be when He looks on us as replicas of Himself– living reflections of **Him**.

> "The Lord your God is in your midst; a mighty one who will save; he will rejoice over you with gladness; he will quiet you by His love; he will exult over you with loud singing..." (Zephaniah 17:17).

The all-powerful, victorious, exulting God sings loudly for joy– over *you.* You, who were weak, confused, helpless, hungry, needy, scowling, messy, squalling.

He gives us light and life when we were in the darkness of our trespasses and sins; He forgives us, washing us clean; He picks us up when we fall, feeds us when we are hungry, protects us, defends us, teaches us His ways– and rejoices over us with great joy. God rejoices with great gladness when He looks at you and sees a living reflection of **Himself.**

> "See what great love the Father has lavished on us, that we should be called children of God! And that is what we are." (1 John 3:1)

What love! What truly amazing love that we have been born again as children of the living God.

CHAPTER 3
Life Begins With Identity

After all these many years, I still remember so well the precise moment when I wondered for the first time if I might be growing a baby. Was I imagining symptoms of morning sickness? Was it just wishful thinking?

My first obstetrical appointment confirmed my suspicion. I told the nurse that I thought maybe I was experiencing some symptoms of pregnancy, but I wasn't sure if that's what it was.

Sympathetically, she asked, "Do you want to have a baby?"

With my young husband finishing his last year in college, she obviously could perceive that we were barely getting by on a shoe-string. Still, I answered her question with what seemed obvious: "Of course I do!"

Her face immediately changed from concern and she smiled a broad, sly grin as she announced, "Well, you are!"

In a kind of stunned elation, Dan and I went back to our student apartment a block from the college and celebrated with a dinner of hot dogs, mustard, relish, and chopped onions. We kept the news to ourselves for awhile, bound together with a secret that seemed too sacred to share with anybody else just yet.

In time, we told family and friends, and the jolting new chapter of motherhood was well on its way. With intense eagerness, I tracked the growth and development of the life inside me. And truthfully, it was breathtaking to witness the creative power of God at work in me.

Life begins at conception. In fact, conception is the greatest miracle of God's infinite creativity that we actually get to participate in. David's Psalm 139 succeeded in expressing the awe of it all when he sang,

> "For you formed my inward parts; you knitted me together in my mother's womb. I praise you for I am fearfully and wonderfully made. Wonderful are your works; my soul knows it very well.
>
> My frame was not hidden from you, when I was being made in secret, intricately woven in the depths of the earth.
>
> Your eyes saw my unformed substance, in your book were written every one of them, the days that were formed for me, when as yet there was none of them.
>
> How precious to me are your thoughts, O God! How vast is the sum of them!" (Psalm 139:13-17)

Among all the glorious revelations of God's infinite power in the universe, the formation of a baby so perfectly displays it.

We tend to think of God's 'infinite nature' only in terms of time; that is, He has no beginning and no end. And yet His infinite nature is most clearly evident in His creation. Try to think back to summer evenings long ago, stretching out on blankets in the backyard in the darkness of night– as we did when our children were young– enthusiastically watching a shower of meteors flash across the sky one after the other. Stunning, bright constellations clearly define the patterns of stars we can see, and the foggy Milky Way gives evidence of more stars than we could possibly count. Clearly, we just have to look up into the vastness of the sky at night to become overwhelmed with God's infinity.

We know now that there is not just one, but there are multiple galaxies in the heavens above– more stars than can be humanly counted in systems that are far beyond our comprehension. Man cannot yet know just how infinitely vast God's creation is.

At the same time, we marvel at the intricate details that man is still in the process of trying to track with our limited human comprehension– tiny molecules made up of atoms which are made up of protons, neutrons, and electrons; the human body made up of cells, and cells containing tiny chains of minuscule DNA–deoxyribonucleic acid– that are themselves made up of even tinier nucleotides that are composed of cytosine, guanine, adenine, and thymine.

If all the DNA could be gathered up from every living human on the earth right now, the total would comprise the size of just a couple of aspirin tablets. [10] It's that small!

---

[10] As per Robert L. Sassone, *The Tiniest Humans*, (American Life League, 1995); quoted by Joni Eareckson Tada in *Heaven: Your Real Home*, (Grand Rapids, Michigan, Zondervan, 1995), 37

How incomprehensibly infinite God's creation is when we look in both directions, farther and farther outwardly and closer and closer inwardly. Is there even a beginning? Or an end? Or is His creation truly infinite?

We know now that a baby does not come from "nothing." In the natural course of God's great design as it was meant to be, in a cellular world so small that it's invisible to the human eye, a multitude of sperm from the father race toward the unfertilized egg at the precise time of a mother's ovulation.

Of the thousands of sperm, only one reaches and penetrates the single cell of the egg, then immediately blocks the egg from any further penetration. In a 2016 report, researchers at the Northwest University in Chicago confirmed that a flash of light occurs at that moment of conception, marking the viability of this fertilization. At that precise moment, zinc is released and binds to tiny molecules that emit a fluorescence, creating an explosion of tiny sparks that appear to be a fluorescent display of fireworks.[11] Life begins with that flash of life-affirming light.

Immediately, half of the mother's chromosomes mesh with half of the father's chromosomes, and a completely new set of DNA is formed– that minuscule chain of intricately detailed data within the cell that is unique to that particular individual. There is no one in the world exactly like this new creation, and never has there ever been. Every detail of that forming child is determined and is already set in place within that chain of DNA. A complex volume of detailed information

---

[11] Kelsey Straeter, *Internet post on Faith It,* (May 1, 2019.)

about who that child is, as well as the history of where he has come from, is contained within that single cell.

Not long ago, I had my DNA tested. After sending the lab nothing more than a sort of Q-tip I had rubbed against the inside of my mouth, the results pin-pointed my heritage with remarkable precision as being from the western area of Ukraine, centering on the Ukraine/Poland border – where I knew that my parents had been born. I felt giddy, stunned as I remembered my Dad, whose birth certificate indicated he was born in Poland, insisting that he was Ukrainian. He had explained to us numerous times that the border had changed back and forth, and though he was Ukrainian, the place where he was born was part of Poland at that time– a detail that confirmed the precise information that I saw reflected in my DNA results.

With absolutely no knowledge of who I am, apart from my husband's Mennonite last name that I carry, my DNA was identified as a very close match to my oldest sister who had taken the DNA test seven years before, whom the test indicated was my closest relative, my sibling– out of thousands, perhaps millions of random participants. That much precise information is contained so perfectly in a chain so tiny that it's completely invisible to the human eye.

That test stirred me. It revealed the incomprehensibly infinite nature of the Creator in a very personal way, the masterful artwork of intelligent design. How absolutely mind-boggling the infinite nature of our God is. What truly breathtaking detail.

At the very moment of conception, each child's genetic makeup, including the sex, is complete, contained within his very own individual chain of DNA. I cannot change my sex any more than I can change my Ukrainian lineage, my brown eyes, my AB- blood type, or the color of my skin. These details are all written within each person's DNA. The child's DNA has similarities to his mother's DNA, and yet he is distinct even from her. He is his own unique person with a very distinct identity. The baby is in his mother's body, but is not part of her body, just as we are in the world, but not part of the world.

The child's personhood does not begin when he takes his first breath; it does not even begin when his heartbeat is initially detected. It begins at the very beginning, at the moment of conception– defined by his DNA, the unique, complex data containing every minute detail of where he has come from, of who he is, and about who this very unique individual will become. Personhood begins with established identity, written within the volumes of his own DNA.

The cell then divides rapidly and repeatedly as it makes its journey into the uterus of the mother where it will attach itself and remain, protected and nourished by the mother as this developing child grows until he is fully formed. A placenta, attached to the child by an umbilical cord, develops in order to transfer nutrients from the mother to the growing child.

In the second trimester, facial features develop; arms, legs, fingers, toes, and eyes are forming. The brain, spinal cord, and nerve tissue of the central nervous system are all well formed.

This second trimester is an active time as the digestive tract and sensory organs develop, and bone begins to replace cartilage. By about six weeks, the heart beat can be detected.

By the end of the third month, the baby is fully developed and needs only time and nutrition in order to mature. Growth and maturity are completely outside of the child's control; they are totally dependent upon the nourishment, life-flow, protection, and care of the mother as he remains in her until the time of fulfillment, the moment he is born into the world.

A continuing debate attempts to alter the determination of when life begins, but we already know the answer. It begins at the flash of light that marks conception. It begins at the very beginning.

Since our life in Christ is the true reality that a child in utero points to, we might wonder when it is that our life in Christ begins. Just as the baby's life begins with that flash of light, and the immediate formation of his DNA – the identity of who he is– our life in Christ also begins with the powerful and magnificent touch of God upon us, that flash of the Light of Christ that reveals our sin and leads us to repentance and belief in the Lord Jesus Christ. At that moment, our identity is secure as children of God.

A baby is conceived through the act of his parents, and does nothing to initiate his own conception. Spiritually, we likewise receive God's life in us through His grace revealed to us by the work of the Holy Spirit in our hearts. We can do nothing to earn it or initiate it. We are incapable of creating such life. It's only by His grace alone through faith alone in Christ alone that His life is breathed into our souls.

At the moment of our spiritual conception– that is, our salvation– our identity is firmly established in Christ. We are His. We may not look much like Him yet, but at the very moment that we believe in Him, we are in Him. This is the truest reality we will ever know.

Salvation itself is not the pinnacle of our Christian experience. It's the starting point. It's our spiritual conception. We were saved by God for His own glory, and the work of sanctification– of being transformed into His image, reflecting His glory to those around us– is just beginning.
R.J.Rushdoony wrote,

> "Salvation is not the goal of faith, but its starting point... Man does not then make salvation the be-all and end-all of religion, but rather the starting point of service, obedience, and enjoyment of God."[12]

The newly conceived baby does not have to look mature in order to be considered alive and human. He is in the process of being formed into the image of his parent until the time he is birthed into the world. Likewise, a newly converted Christian hardly looks like the fully formed image of Christ that he will eventually be.

---

[12] R.J.Rushdoony, *Commentary of Romans and Galatians,* (Vallecito, California, Ross House Publishing, 1997), 58, 59.

From the moment of our spiritual conception, we are growing– growing more and more into the image of God. We are being shaped and formed through various experiences, trials, joys, adversities, successes, failures, and victories for that day when we will see Him face to face. We are being prepared for eternal life in the Son. When we see Him, we will be fully formed, just as the baby will be fully formed when, upon birth, he finally sees his mother.

Our spiritual maturity is not something we can boast about, as though it's dependent upon anything we ourselves can control. If we are truly in Christ, it's by His life in us that we are changed more and more into His image, molded into what He wants us to be.

A baby in utero is sustained by the life and nourishment of his mother; we in Christ are sustained, protected, held by God. He has promised to complete what He has begun in us, and so He will.

Life begins at conception– both physically and spiritually. It begins at the moment when we are marked with our identity. From that moment on, we find our life in Him as we are shaped into His image.

> "All things were made through Him, and without Him was not anything made that was made. In Him was life, and the life was the light of men," (John 1:3,4).

CHAPTER 4

Born, and Then Born Again

Birth is the greatest miracle we can know on this earth.

Okay, let me repeat that, but this time I'll say it a little louder to make sure you don't miss it: **Birth is the greatest miracle we can know on this earth!**

It's also one of the greatest teachers that points us to Christ and to our entrance into His everlasting Kingdom. From what appears to come from nothing–a mere breath of life growing into a perfectly formed human being who is a living soul–birth is absolutely awe inspiring. Ecclesiastes 11:5 is such a good expression of this great mystery:

> "As you do not know the way the spirit comes to the bones in the womb of a woman with child, so you do not know the work of God who makes everything."

What a mystery!

Nothing in the universe, as wonderful as it all is, can so eloquently speak of the glory of God like the miracle of conception and birth. Nothing points to the power, the sovereignty, the creativity, the purposes of God so precisely. Multiple times, the Bible refers to birth, calling us "children of God." It's no wonder that the whole message of the Gospel is wrapped up in the birth, death, and resurrection of Jesus, the promised Messiah who left heaven's glory and came to earth–entered "the womb of heaven" through Mary's womb– and was birthed as a baby in human form in order to make God known to us as we identify with Him through new birth.

Just like newborn babes, we who are weak, helpless, hungry, needy are embraced by God with such deep and incomprehensible love that ironically, we have done nothing to deserve. And yet while we were still in our weakness and sin, He loved us, and sent Jesus who willingly gave His life for ours so that in believing, we could inherit His Kingdom– that is, belong to His family, be called by His name.

Clearly, to leave an infant alone is to essentially kill it, and it is exactly the same with us. Left without God– physically as well as spiritually– we die.

Apart from God, we cannot sustain our own life, and there is nothing we can do of our own strength or ability in order to enter His Kingdom. Christ did it all. He alone is our protection, our nourishment, our sustenance, our life. Separated from God, we die both physically and spiritually.

And yet God, through His mercy gives life through His Son. He sent Jesus to be born as a baby, to live a life we can identify with, to suffer as He bore our sins in order to give the sure hope of eternal life to all who believe in Him.

Near the end of the book of John, the writer related the purpose for which he'd written his record of Jesus' time on earth:

> "These things are written so that you may *believe* that Jesus is the Christ, the Son of God, and that *by believing,* you may have life in his name," (John 20:31).

Believing that there is a God (or a god) is one thing; but *what* we believe about Him is quite another.

He gives us fullness of life when we *believe* that all things were created by Him and for Him, and that in Him all things hold together. He gives us life when we *believe* that Jesus Christ is the Son of God who came to earth, died for our sins, was resurrected, and ascended back to the Father. He gives life when we *believe* that all authority in heaven and in earth is His alone.

And yet we can't strive to believe, or force it to happen apart from the work of the Holy Spirit to convict us of our sin and open our blind eyes. We believe **in Him.**

To believe is to accept something as true. I believe, of course, that this is a chair that's holding me up as I write this. I don't have to convince myself to believe it. I believe it, or I don't. And yet, strive as I might, I can't force myself to believe that this chair is the throne of the Queen of England if it isn't. Belief is not the power of positive thinking– of trying to change our reality and make something happen by our own effort.

Belief is the sure knowledge that something is true, whether we see it or not. I believe there is a massive galaxy in the sky above, though I can't see it. I believe there is a marine world teaming with life just under the surface of the ocean, though I can't see it. I believe that my son and his family are living vibrant, active lives on the other side of this continent, though I can't see them. I believe that there is an actual baby growing in the womb of his mother, though I can't see him. I believe that Jesus is the Son of God who died to pay the penalty for my sin, was resurrected, and is seated right now on His Father's throne, exercising all authority in heaven and on earth, though I can't see Him.

Just as the baby in utero begins as merely a single cell, belief also begins in primitive form. It may not begin as very much, but it's truly the seed of what it will become– and its growth is not our responsibility, but God's as we live in Him.

Mark 9 records the story of a father whose heart was aching to see his son healed of his affliction in convulsing. When Jesus told him that all things were possible for one who believes, the father's response to Him was, "I believe; help my unbelief!" His belief was in seed form, not yet what it would fully become, and yet Jesus honored it. So it is with us. It's by the power of God Himself that our belief in Him grows– as we live and move and have our being in Him. We believe even what we can't see; and our humble prayer is always that God, by His power, would help our unbelief.

We can't see the baby forming in utero, but we believe the process of how it happens. Neither can we see God, but we believe in Him through Jesus His Son. Like the baby in utero who does not strive in order to grow, we do not have to strive in order to find life in the Life-Giver as we abide in Him. We believe that Jesus is indeed His Son who came into the dark confines of earth– into the "womb of heaven," and took our sins upon Himself to make the way for us to approach God. In believing, we find forgiveness of our sins and are born into everlasting life.

When Jesus was a man on earth, He Himself used the miracle of birth as the picture that best communicated to Nicodemus the miracle of our entrance into the Kingdom of God– made alive in Christ.

> "'Truly I say to you, unless one is born again, he cannot see the kingdom of God.'
>
> Nicodemus said to him, 'How can a man be born when he is old? Can he enter a second time into his mother's womb and be born?'
>
> Jesus answered, 'Truly, truly I say to you, unless one is born of water and the Spirit, he cannot enter the kingdom of God. That which is born of the flesh is flesh, and that which is born of the Spirit is spirit. Do not marvel that I said to you, You must be born again.'" (John 3:3-8)

Like the newborn baby who emerges out of the darkness into brightness and color and beauty, 1 Peter 2:9 says that He has called us out of darkness into his marvelous light. Brought out of the darkness of our sin and selfishness, we become children of God through new birth.

The baby does not strive to be born. His mother does all the work. But neither can he, of his own volition, refuse to be born. He is pushed along by the force of his mother's effort, even though it may be very uncomfortable– even painful– for the baby during the process. Similarly, once the reality of God's Son Jesus has been revealed to you by His Holy Spirit, you simply can't refuse to believe.

Admittedly, it may not initially be very comfortable to realize how transforming this change will be. It may be quite painful! And those birth pains can be intense. It may very well be frightening to realize you must leave the comfort of the dark, confined sphere of everything you knew before as familiar.

One of the most eye-opening stories of new birth is in the book, The Secret Thoughts of an Unlikely Convert by Rosaria Butterfield. This author described her conversion to the Christian faith as "a train wreck," because she knew that every comfortable, secure detail of her past life had ended– her identity as a lesbian, her relationship with her lesbian lover, the house they owned together, her large group of ungodly friends, her career as an outspoken professor of women's rights at a liberal university. Still, she knew that all of it had to be left behind in the darkness when she was born again, because she was convinced of the Truth, and it was impossible to *not* believe in the reality of Christ Jesus.

Once you believe, the change– like childbirth– simply can't be stopped, and the new life in Christ is powerfully greater. You truly understand that to have remained in that old womb would only have meant continuing darkness, confinement, and ultimate death.

In his book Surprised by Joy, C.S. Lewis wrote about his conversion, that once his eyes were opened to the harsh reality of the darkness he was living in– "a bedlam of ambitions, a nursery of fears, a harem of fondled hatreds"[13]– there was no question that the reality of God through Jesus Christ was real, and there was simply no turning back to the darkness.

Just as varied and complex as natural birth experiences are, so are the experiences of new birth. Some are birthed quickly and seemingly effortlessly; others with much resistance, difficulty, and struggle; some take a long time to be delivered; a few even require surgical intervention; some seem almost uneventful, while others are quite dramatic. Lewis wrote about the relentless push of "...Him whom I so earnestly desired not to meet..." until finally "...I gave in, and admitted that God was God and knelt and prayed: perhaps, that night, the most dejected and reluctant convert in all England..." Yet ultimately, Lewis concluded that, "The hardness of God is kinder than the softness of men, and His compulsion is our liberation."[14]

There is only one way to true liberation: through 'new birth,' even when it initially seems painful.

Jesus had told Nicodemus that there was only one way into the Kingdom of Heaven: through new birth. We understand

---

[13] C.S.Lewis, *Surprised by Joy, (New York, Harcourt Brace Jovanovich Publishers, 1955) 226*

[14] Ibid *228, 229*

that because there is only one way into the world: through the awe-inspiring miracle of birth.

When birth requires a harsh surgery, as in a C-Section, the healing takes time and great care, but ultimately it produces unfathomable life and strength.

Birth is such a breathtaking picture of our miraculous re-birth into Christ, and the truly amazing way in which He nourishes us, protects us, and shapes us to be more and more like Him as we grow in Him.

Let me say this just one more time: birth *is* the greatest miracle we can know on this earth!

CHAPTER 5
Heaven's Womb

If you didn't already know this little tidbit of information, you might find it interesting to know that a mother elephant carries her baby for almost 22 months before giving birth. A mouse, on the other hand, carries its young for a mere 19 days before the mischief is born. Yes, a group of mice is called a "mischief." No surprise there. But this helps to put some perspective into the nine months that a human mother carries her young before birth, given the incredible amount of detail involved in the formation of a human baby- and much more significantly, a living soul.

For nine months, a baby remains in his mother's womb, growing, becoming more and more like her in image and function. There is a significant purpose for the baby's nine months of growth in utero: every single detail of the baby's growth and development is perfectly designed by our Creator God in order to prepare him for life in the world.

The funny thing is, even as he is in the dark confines of the womb, the baby is in the world, is surrounded by the world, and is even part of the world– but he has not been released into it yet. He is in the process of being formed for the day when he will be born. Every part of his growth is designed to prepare and equip him to live in the new environment.

The development of his heart, his lungs, his digestive tract, his circulatory system, his skeleton– every intricate detail of his body is woven together with precision in order to prepare him for life in the world after he is born. Every detail is.

Think about the way his blood coagulates– it's such a seemingly minor detail of his development, and yet without it, he would struggle to survive in the world. Or think about his immune system, or his skin's ability to heal, or the perfect placement of his fingers and thumb. Thousands of such details are being woven together in those nine months– the clear artwork of intelligent design– in order to equip him for life on this earth.

And yet there's a far greater purpose than living on this present earth.

Just as the child was created in order to live and function in the world when he is eventually released into it, we being in Christ are also being prepared for the ultimate purpose of living in His everlasting Kingdom, which is our destiny. And yet His Kingdom is not somewhere separate from where we are now. We're part of His Kingdom now; we're surrounded by it now– but we have not yet been born into the fullness of it.

Catholic theologian and philosopher Peter Kreeft has said,

> "To medieval Christiandom...earth was Heaven's womb, Heaven's nursery, Heaven's dress rehearsal. Heaven was the meaning of the earth."[15]

---

15 Peter Kreeft, article *What Difference Does Heaven Make*, (Integrated Catholic Life, 2012)

"Heaven's womb." The child in utero is an exact reflection of our entrance into the Kingdom of Heaven. Thinkers and theologians have long considered earth as 'heaven's womb,' uniting earth and heaven together as the Kingdom of Heaven-as it should be.

Earth is not the best of our existence. It's merely the womb of heaven. Earth as we currently know it is not the ultimate fulfillment of what we were created for. We were made for eternity. That's what's in our hearts and minds, and certainly in our affections. C.S.Lewis wrote,

> "If I find in myself a desire which no experience in this world can satisfy, the most probable explanation is that I was made for another world...Earthly pleasures were never meant to satisfy it, but only to arouse it, to suggest the real thing." [16]

For too long, we've thought of heaven as somewhere far away, distinct from earth. From the time we're toddlers, we think of heaven as up there somewhere, someplace separate from earth– as though earth and heaven were two individual, distinct realms functioning independently of each other, separated by a lot of space.

But that isn't so.

We might even erroneously imagine heaven to be a sort of "dream world," with no real substance– just wispy forms of

---

[16] C.S.Lewis, *Mere Christianity,* (Harper Collins Publishers, 1952 reprinted 1980) 136-137

nebulous beings floating around somewhere, invisible to the human eye. But that isn't so either.

Heaven is real and substantive. It's not less than we know, it's far, far more than what we know on earth. All of our realities here on earth will be evident in heaven, plus more.

Right now, in the darkness of the womb of heaven, we can only know three dimensions plus time, which strictly confine us. Writer Peter Kreeft wrote,

> "Time is a line, as the West knows, progressing in a single direction from past to future, from birth to death, from creation to the end of the world, from a real and absolute beginning to a real and absolute ending..."[17]

But then, in order to help us grasp the greater picture of what God Himself sees, and what we will eventually know in the greater dimensions of eternity, he continued,

> "The point (eternity) is off the line (time), not one of the many moving points on it. It is transcendent. But it is also immanent in the whole line; in fact, it is the line looked at end-on. This is why God's eternal eye looking at our lives end-on from the point of their consummating perfection can say to us radically imperfect creatures in time: 'Behold, you are all fair, my love; there is no spot or wrinkle in you'... From this

---

[17] Peter Kreeft, *Heaven, the Heart's Deepest Longing*, (Ignatius Publishing, 1989) 90

> God's-eye point of view, 'all things work together for good for those who love God, those who are called according to his purpose.'[18]

Consequently as creatures who are confined to the dimension of time here on earth, we often slide into imagining heaven in a chronological setting, as though when Jesus ascended, everything in heaven froze into the setting of biblical times– like wearing robes styled after those worn by Jesus and His disciples, or speaking the language of the King James era.

In truth, it's as impossible for us to imagine what heaven must be like as it is for a baby to imagine the world he is going to be birthed into. In the womb, it's dark, warm, and very much confined. But the baby feels secure and snug. He feels his mother's heartbeat, and hears her voice. It's all he knows, and he is content.

He could never in his wildest dreams imagine the world he will be born into. As he enters it, he is immediately swallowed up by incredible brightness, color, sounds, lights, smells. As he grows, he discovers flowers– not just one flower, but thousands of different kinds– an amazing variety of animals, foods of a wide variety of tastes and textures; water, sky, clouds, stars; music, people, and space. What an extreme change!

That's what it will be like when we are born into heaven.

[18] Ibid, p. 86, 87

Not long ago, I asked some of my grandkids how many colors they thought might be in heaven. That's a hard question, because colors here on earth seem infinite. In truth, the average person can normally see about a whopping million different colors (you'll be convinced this is true when you look for samples of 'white' at the paint store), so it's definitely hard to even imagine there could possibly be more than that.

All the colors we know derive from only three primary colors. But what if there are more than three primary colors in heaven? In that case, there will be colors we have never even imagined!

Soon after I had that conversation, I discovered that there are individuals who are tetrachromatic– who see a hundred times more colors than the normal person can see. The average person possesses three cones or channels for conveying color information. However, rarely there are individuals– tetrachromats– who have four channels, enabling them to see a hundred times more colors. A hundred times more colors!

There are more colors than what we know. We just don't have the capacity to even imagine the variety of colors there will be in heaven.

We won't have to give up the realities of what we know here on earth when we get to heaven. It's completely the opposite! There are more dimensions, more senses, more colors, more variety, more functions... more of everything.

Unfortunately, much of my childhood is a foggy blur as I was born with very poor vision. My stubborn Ukrainian father had perfect vision and found it incomprehensible that a child wouldn't be able to see, so he refused to consider the school nurse's persistent urging to have my eyes tested. To him, poor vision was solely the result of aging. Consequently, I was already a young teenager when I finally got my first pair of corrective glasses, old enough that the memory is emblazoned in my memory. Foolishly, I stood in the optometrist's waiting room, mesmerized by the pattern on the oriental carpet. Just staring at it! Eventually, my gaze shifted to the window, and again, I stood in utter wonder staring down at the street scene below from the second floor. What clarity! What detail I had missed! There was a whole new dimension of life that had slipped by totally unnoticed!

Life in the womb of heaven is very much like that. As we are formed into His image, things become more clear, and yet we're still so limited in what we can see. When we are born into heaven, everything will be clear.

> "For now we see through a glass, darkly; but then face to face: now I know in part; but then shall I know even as also I am known," (1 Corinthians 13:12.)

As someone who grew up with very blurry vision, terrible allergies that kept my head in a fog, as well as increasingly worse hearing issues as I've aged, I look very much forward to the mental and physical acuteness that will be mine in heaven. Heaven will be all the reality I can experience here, but with far greater clarity and alertness.

Here, our bodies need to recharge every night, and sometimes we struggle to function because of insufficient sleep– but in heaven, we will be fully charged and wider awake than we've ever been in our lives here.

Heaven surrounds us, and it's much closer than we can imagine– but it's in a dimension we cannot access right now. Like the baby in utero who is prevented from seeing the world that surrounds him, even though he is part of it and the physical reality of it is merely inches away from him, we are likewise prevented from seeing heaven until we will be born into it.

Even now, we are in the Kingdom of Heaven, we are surrounded by the Kingdom of Heaven, and we are part of the Kingdom of Heaven. But we haven't been fully released into it yet. We have only a mere glimpse of it, a downpayment of our full inheritance (see Ephesians 1:13, 14.)

A baby in utero could never imagine that he is within mere inches of this amazing world he will be born into. Likewise, we are surrounded by heaven, and it's so close. We just can't see it yet. Only a veil, or a curtain, separates us from the full reality of heaven.

The Old Testament tabernacle is a picture that helps us understand this. The Most Holy Place of the tabernacle was where the physical presence of God was, and was separated from the rest of the tabernacle merely by an inaccessible curtain. It was a picture of the heavenly presence of God, separated for us by a mere curtain– a dimension we do not yet have access to. Hebrews 9: 24 says,

> "For Christ has entered, not into holy places made with hands, which are copies of the true things, but into heaven itself, now to appear in the presence of God on our behalf."

Long ago, evangelist and publisher D.L.Moody said,

> "One day you will read in the papers that Moody is dead. Don't believe a word of it! At that moment, I will be more alive than I am now. I was born in the flesh in 1837 and I was born of the Spirit in 1855. That which is born of the flesh may die, but that which is born of the Spirit will live forever." [19]

> "We have this as a sure and steadfast anchor of the soul, a hope that enters into the inner place behind the curtain where Jesus has gone as a forerunner on our behalf," (Hebrews 6:19).

---

[19] https://www.christianquotes.info/quotes-by-author/dwight-l-moody-quotes/

CHAPTER 6

Already, But Not Yet

So here's the big question we need to consider: when do we become children of the Kingdom of Heaven? Is it a promise for some future time after we die? Or is it a promise for now?

We know that we belong to God's family, and that by believing in Him we inherit everlasting life. And yet while we are still in this world, we struggle against the power of sin both in us, and around us. We know that we are not a perfect reflection of Christ yet. So at what point do we inherit the Kingdom? Now? Or when we get to heaven?

In our church, we often hear about this quandary as the "already, but not yet" aspect of the Gospel, of being currently active as well as future participants in the Kingdom of God.

1 John 3:2 tells us that:

> "Beloved, we are God's children **now**," and yet, "what we will be **has not yet** appeared; but we know that when he appears we shall be like him, because we shall see him as he is."

We are already [sons], but not yet [what we will be.]

There's a powerfully descriptive picture of "already, but not yet" expressed in C.S. Lewis' Chronicles of Narnia, especially in the story of The Lion, the Witch, and the Wardrobe.[20] The

[20] C.S.Lewis, *The Lion, the Witch, and the Wardrobe,* (New York, Macmillan Publishing Company, 1970)

story tells of four children– Peter, Susan, Edmond, and Lucy– who find themselves in a faraway country of Narnia that can only be accessed through a dimension that's beyond what they'd ever known on earth. Once they enter Narnia through a magic wardrobe, they find that they are kings and queens of Aslan, the powerful and majestic lion who is the rightful ruler of Narnia.

However, until all evil is ultimately destroyed and Narnia is re-created in perfection by Aslan, as earth will be in Christ's final victory, these four have many battles that must be fought as the White Witch strives to usurp Aslan's rule. She knows she is already defeated, but her relentless attack is to bring down as many as she can with her, just as Satan does knowing he is already-but-not-yet defeated.

The children know that they belong in Aslan's royal family and that they will ultimately have full and complete victory– and yet while they are in Narnia, there are battles that must be fought against dark forces.

That's exactly like us. We know who we are. We are members of Christ's royal family, heirs of the Kingdom of Heaven, and the reality of it is evident now. But we have not yet entered heaven, the place without sin. For now, there are battles that must be fought– both within and without– while sin is still in this world. One day, God will recreate the world without sin, and heaven and earth will again be joined as they were in Eden– without sin, without the battles we must fight against the flesh.

We are God's children, heirs of His Kingdom now. We belong to Him now. He is our Father now. Right now, we have access to all that He is, and He has commanded us to exercise His dominion mandate here on the earth as representatives of His Kingdom. We know His peace, His strength, His mercy, His forgiveness now. And yet we will not be fully formed into His image until we are birthed into heaven, when we physically see Him face to face, when we will finally be without sin.

To help us grasp this reality, let's look again at the tiny child, and consider at what point a baby becomes the mother's child. When his lungs first fill with air as he takes his first breath?

Perhaps before that, when his heartbeat is first detected in utero? Or is it even before that, before a mother even begins to recognize the symptoms of pregnancy that herald the awareness that she is growing a baby?

In truth, it is right at the beginning, at conception, when his very own individual data is formed within his chain of DNA–the "seed" of what he is becoming.

A mother begins to love her child and rejoice with a fierce maternal drive to protect and nourish this new life even before the heartbeat is detected. Apart from those times when women are set off course by the hardness of sin (hers, or someone else's), by God's design this intense love for the child explodes upon the mother's realization that a child is growing in her womb.

Miscarriage is an honest testament of the love a mother has for the child even long before he is born. I've experienced the great grief of miscarrying a child in the third month of pregnancy. The tears I wept, and the heavy heart weighed down with grief was a witness to the love I had for the child I was carrying. My husband, children, and I had been so excited when we realized a baby was on the way.

Everyone on the planet has experienced some sort of loss at some point in life, so we all know that the degree of grief we experience when someone dies is commensurate to the degree of love we had for that person. Long before I miscarried the child, I loved him. His life was extremely short, yet for those months, the child was so greatly loved.

Without a doubt, the baby is the mother's child long before he is birthed into the world. God has designed the woman with an instinctive drive to protect her young from the very beginning.

A baby is the mother's child before the mother herself even realizes she has conceived, and unless a woman is deceived by sin, she is driven to love and protect him, long before she can see him.

The book of Jeremiah begins with the affirmation that God knew Jeremiah– He planned his existence, his birth– not only before he was born, but even before he was conceived!

> "Before I formed you in the womb, I knew you, and before you were born I consecrated you; I appointed you a prophet to the nations." (Jeremiah 1:3)

God Himself is the giver of life, and brings life into being at the moment of conception. The child's identity is firmly established immediately, even though he is not yet what he will be. He is "already- but not yet."

What a perfect reflection of how we become children of the living God at the moment of our spiritual conception. Our identity is firmly established, and we are fiercely loved by God– though we have much growing to do while we're still here in the womb of heaven.

One day, we will be released from the darkness of this world– this womb of heaven– and be born into the freedom of eternity. When we see Him, we will be fully formed. We will be like Him. Right now, we are not yet what we will be when we get there, but thanks be to God, we are not what we used to be!

> "Our citizenship is in heaven, and from it we await a Savior, the Lord Jesus Christ, who will transform our lowly body to be like his glorious body," says Philippians 3:20.

We are "already," thanks be to God!

But, of course, we are "not yet."

CHAPTER 7

Made in God's Image

A photo has circulated the Internet of twin babies in utero, with a caption of them wondering over the existence of a mother. One twin asks the other, "Do you believe in Mom?" The second twin responds, "No, of course not! After all, have you ever actually seen her?"

Do you believe in God? After all, you have not actually seen Him, have you?

The mother surrounding the child in utero may seem invisible to him, and yet she is vitally present, very real. She is the source of his life. In the same way, we cannot see God, but we are physically and spiritually surrounded by Him.

He is the very source of our life in much the same way that the life of a vine nourishes the branches of a plant. Where does one begin and the other end? They are interconnected– the vine in the branches, and the branches in the vine– and yet life streams from the vine into the branches. I know this is true because when I prune branches from my raspberry bushes, the branches that disconnect from the source shrivel up and die.

> "As the branch cannot bear fruit by itself, unless it abides in the vine, neither can you, unless you abide in me. I am the vine; you are the branches. Whoever abides in me and I in him, he it is that bears much

> fruit; for apart from me, you can do nothing," said Jesus in John 15:4,5.

God is our life source. His life in us is the "main thing." And yet we perpetually turn our attention away from the main thing, highly distracted by trying to imagine what God *looks* like, as though knowing would somehow satisfy us.

There is only one true God ruling, existing in the Trinity – Father, Son, Holy Spirit. There are not three separate Gods with three separate forms. Jesus is the form of God and has been, all through eternity.

> "[Jesus] is the image of the invisible God...For by him all things were created in heaven and on earth, visible and invisible, whether thrones or dominions or rulers or authorities–all things were created through him and for him," (Colossians 1:15).

Jesus was not merely a created being who came into existence when He was born to Mary as a baby. He always was, having created the world by the Word who later became flesh among us. As the form of God, He stepped out of eternity, and came into our world of time by the will of the Father. And yet He was present with the Father and the Holy Spirit from the very beginning.

At Creation, God said, "Let us make man in our image, after our likeness," (Genesis 1:26). The writer of Hebrews 1: 2 affirms the unity of God the Father, the Son, and the Holy Spirit in the work of Creation when he speaks of Jesus, "through whom also [God the Father] created the world." It was by His Word that all things were brought into being. It was Jesus– the Word made flesh, the very form of God– in whose image man was created.

It's important to understand that at Creation, woman was not an 'after-thought' for God, as though He suddenly realized that His original design wasn't going to work out on his own as well as He'd hoped. In truth, man wasn't going to work out on his own, but God already knew that. Neither did woman work well without the man. He designed them intentionally, from the beginning, to be together forming one complete unit.

God did not suddenly realize that He'd made a mistake He had to correct by going back to the drawing board to think up a subset to His design. He intentionally created man first, and man himself needed to realize that it was not a good thing for him to be alone. From the beginning of time, woman was God's image-bearer along with man, created by God as the completion of man in order to reflect God Himself. Together, they were designed to reproduce– and reproduction is the means by which the Kingdom of God grows. Fruitfulness characterizes His Kingdom.

There was intentional reason in God's creation of man as male and female, two becoming one. After God had created the stage upon which man would live out His assigned purposes on the earth, Genesis 1:26, 27 records that God said,

> "Let us make man in our image, after our likeness... So God created man in his own image, in the image of God he created him; male and female he created them."

Man– that is, male plus female– was created as a complete unit that was made in the image of God. The two became one.

Then God blessed male-plus-female with His assignment, recorded in Genesis 1:28:

> "God blessed them. And God said to them, 'Be fruitful and multiply and fill the earth and subdue it, and have dominion over...every living thing that moves on the earth.'"

God's command for man and woman to have children was a blessing He bestowed upon man.

Together, the male-plus-female, fashioned in the image of God Himself, was designed to "be fruitful and multiply" in order to fulfill God's mandate, and thus be blessed. He repeated this mandate again after the flood (Genesis 8:16,17), and He repeated it again to the exiles in Babylon (Jeremiah 29:6.)

In the book Common Sense 101 Lessons from G.K. Chesterton, author Dale Ahlquist emphasized Chesterton's constant attempts to urge others in a return to 'first principles.' He quoted Chesterton saying,

> "We shall never return to social sanity till we begin at the beginning. We must start where all history starts, with a man and a woman, and a child, and with the province of liberty and property which these need for their full humanity. As it is, we begin where history

> ends... We judge everything by the particular muddle of the moment." [21]

We are witnessing this muddle of the moment as man's great temptation is– and has always been– to squeeze God into our image. Because we can't see Him, all through history man has perpetually tried to create an image of what God looks like, as though man were the standard by which God ought to conform. Think again of how this idea was expressed by those twin babies in utero referred to in the beginning of this chapter.

Man has always sought to create an image of God that can be understood or easily imagined by our own limited minds. We've imagined God to be a jolly old elf in a red suit. Or a stern old man with a long white beard and a staff, scowling at us as He sits on the edge of an ancient throne. Or a big black Mama called 'Papa.' There's a word for this practice of forming God into a human image like us so that we can relate to Him in our terms: "anthropomorphism." It makes God like us, instead of us being made like God.

"The religions of Paul's day were anthropomorphic," wrote R.J.Rushdoony as he considered the book of Galatians,

> "i.e., they remade their god or gods in man's image. As a result, what was predicted of man had to be predicted of the gods...If man is anthropomorphic in

---

[21] Dale Ahlquist, *Common Sense 101: Lessons from G.K. Chesterton*, (San Francisco, Ignatius Press, 2006) 146

> his religion, he ascribes to God a mentality like his own: he remakes God in his own human image."22

From earliest times, men have wrestled with wondering, what does our Father God look like?

Even Jesus' disciples struggled with this.

> "Philip said to him, 'Lord, show us the Father, and it is enough for us.' Jesus said to him, 'Have I been with you so long, and you still do not know me, Philip? Whoever has seen me has seen the Father. How can you say, 'Show us the Father'?'" (John 14:8-10)

We constantly strive to imagine God the Father as though He were made in our image. And yet refusing to believe in God unless He conforms to the same size, shape, or mentality as we are is as silly as the yet-unrecognizable pre-born child– like the twin mentioned above– who is still in the process of being formed, still far from what he will eventually be, refusing to believe in his mother because she isn't the same size and form as he, the fetus, is.

That froggy-looking still-being-formed embryo in utero may not look very "human" yet, but is growing more and more into the human image of his parent. From the moment of his conception, he was created in the image of his parent even while he is still in the womb, even while he is still in the process of being formed and shaped. When he is fully formed

---

[22] R.J.Rushdoony, *[Commentary on] Romans and Galatians,* (Vallecito, CA, Ross House Publishers, 1997) 381, 383

and birthed, he will look completely human. He will be like her.

That child– and every human child who enters the womb– has been made in the image of God. In Matthew 18:10 Jesus told His disciples:

> "See that you do not despise one of these little ones. For I tell you that in heaven their angels always see the face of my Father who is in heaven."

Set apart from every other living form in the world that was spoken into existence by God at Creation, the human has been fashioned by the very hand of God to reflect the glorious and sacred image of God revealed in His Son Jesus Christ, then given life by the very breath of God in order to create for Himself a living soul.

In this same way, while we're still in the womb of heaven we are being shaped into the image of God as we live in Him– nourished, protected, sustained by His life in us. There is so much more to Him than our present minds could possibly comprehend! We are so limited by what we know right now.

We are His. We are completely in Him. We were created in His image and in His likeness. Our minds right now do not have the capacity to fully know the greatness of who God is any more than the forming baby in utero can fully know his mother.

And yet God has made Himself known to us through His Son Jesus, the Word made flesh, who was fully God and fully man.

At this very moment, Jesus is sitting at the throne of heaven in a physical glorified body that is human in form, and He intercedes to the Father on our behalf.

In John 20:29 Jesus gently rebuked Thomas for saying he would not believe in a resurrected Jesus unless he could *see* Him. Jesus said to him, "Blessed are those who have not seen, and yet have believed."

While we're here on this earth, we must be content knowing that God is the constant source of our strength, our growth, our formation, our protection. That's the 'main thing.'

We were created in His image even as we are still in the continuing process of being *formed* into His image. We may not look very much like Him yet, but when we see Jesus, when we are birthed into heaven, we will be fully formed. We will see Him as He is. And we will be like Him.

> "Beloved, we are God's children now, and what we will be has not yet appeared; but we know that when he appears we shall be like him, because we shall see him as he is." (1 John 3:2)

CHAPTER 8

Transformation, the Sign of Life

It was inevitable, I suppose, that one of my grandkids would eventually want to raise rabbits because every child wants to raise rabbits. So as his eleventh birthday approached, Ethan expressed his strong wish for a couple of rabbits, and sure enough, his parents surprised him with them.

As you've already guessed, it didn't take long for these rabbits to multiply– which was likewise inevitable– and just a couple of weeks ago, Ethan was ecstatic to discover that his mother rabbit had given birth to a litter of six baby bunnies.

I think rabbits are a gift from God so that He can amaze us over how quickly they transform, almost before our very eyes. It's like watching the creative hand of God at work. Rabbits, you know, have a mere gestation period of only one month, and consequently, they arrive looking like they are still in process. At birth– just a couple of weeks ago– these bunnies were tiny, naked, quivering, blind, pathetic little creatures huddling together under a nest of soft fur their momma bunny had sacrificially constructed for them out of her own coat.

But within merely days, these little critters began to grow fur of their own, and one by one, their eyes began to open, even as they each hobbled their way to momma's milk supply. By the end of just a couple of weeks, they had become true rabbits, fully coated with their own distinct markings of fur, fully functional as they hopped around full of life, looking for food.

All around us, we are literally surrounded by innumerable evidences of life, so perfectly detailed by a most powerful Creator God. And yet nowhere is that creative power as evident to us as we see it in the transformation of a baby in utero, the clear witness that there is life.

From a single cell, the child in utero grows swiftly and develops at a rapid pace. If there were no growth or change, it would indicate that there was no life, and therefore the cell– or fetus or child– would eventually be miscarried. He cannot remain the same and stay in his mother's womb.

Growth and transformation are the clear indications of life. Size does not matter; if even a single cell is dividing, growing and transforming, it's evidence that there is life. Clearly, life in the womb begins at conception, at that moment when a single cell begins the process of transformation. Growth cannot take place without life, even from a single cell. If there is growth, then there is life. A baby in the womb is never merely a "clump of 'lifeless' cells." To try to differentiate life in the womb from a "clump of cells" is an oxymoron. There cannot be a clump of growing cells unless it has life.

The Kingdom of God is marked by the same thing: healthy transformation. If there is no growth, it is obvious that there is no life. But if there is change and growth, then clearly, there is life.

Without Christ, we are dead in our trespasses and sins (Ephesians 2:1); but when we have been made alive in Him (Ephesians 2:5), there is clear evidence of growth and change. Just as the child in utero is always being transformed more and more into the image of his parents, so we being in Christ are being changed more and more into the image of God.

> "We all, with unveiled face beholding the glory of the Lord are being transformed into the same image from one degree of glory to another," (2 Corinthians 3:18).

My own conversion to faith in Christ Jesus convinces me of this. In my high school years, I struggled with a very poor self-image, insecurity over who I was, confusion over what I believed, and ensuing depression. Waking one morning deeply discouraged, I cried out to God in a prayer of desperation that if He was really real, as my parents believed He was, then I begged for Him to change me. I just could not bear the thought of continuing to drift mindlessly through my whole life with the never-changing internal tension I continued to experience.

Strangely enough, considering the intensity of that prayer, I completely forgot about it. That is, until one day many years later, when my circumstances had totally changed. I was newly married, strongly enthusiastic in the faith, confident of my identity in Christ Jesus, eager to live life and experience all that He had for my husband and me.

At that time, Dan and I were on a two-month-long mission trip to Jamaica. After spending a long, hard day laying bricks for a nationals' Bible School building in a tiny village called

"Time and Patience," Dan was preaching to a small congregation in a primitive back country structure outside of Kingston that served as a church. The building had a noisy tin roof, and there were large open spaces where windows should have been. There were no doors, and chickens kept wandering in and out of the structure, even as we sang hymns and prayed.

As I sat listening to my husband speaking, a very strange thing happened. It suddenly seemed as though a movie began to play in front of me, and out of nowhere, in my mind I saw a picture of myself crying out to God years before. Out of total oblivion, the memory came with acute clarity. For years, I had completely forgotten all about it, until that moment.

At the same time, I *saw* that God had changed me. He had answered my desperate prayer, though I don't know how or when it had happened. He had blinded my eyes to what He was doing until this moment when I knew, without a doubt, that God had transformed my life. Through absolutely no effort of my own, I was changed by God Himself!

When I had witnessed the transformation within myself– something that had been completely outside of my own control– the reality of God and His transforming power were undeniable. I knew without a doubt that His life was in me, and I knew I was in Him.

Understanding the vitality of life that transformation brings is what defines the great divide between the Kingdom of Heaven which is Light and the kingdom of the world system which is darkness. A dark world bears a message of death and barrenness as it seeks to kill off pre-born babies at an astounding rate, and promotes the concept of same-sex marriage that defies reproduction– trying desperately to convince us that our own personal happiness is all that matters, at whatever the cost to those around us. And now, we've witnessed the onslaught of a strange, manufactured virus that is predominantly killing the older generation. We should be shocked, but we shouldn't be surprised: this is the character of a kingdom of death and barrenness.

The Kingdom of Heaven, on the other hand, is characterized by a gospel message of life and fruitfulness. We see it both in ourselves and in others around us. Life is characterized by transformation. We are growing, producing, transforming, becoming more like Christ. If we are truly **in Christ,** we are not what we used to be. It's useless to dig up offenses from the past except to repent of them, because we know that we are not the same people we were back then. It would likewise be pointless– in fact, sinful– for me to dig up offenses that I had perceived in my husband 45 years ago, because he is not the same man I married back then. Thanks be to God that he can say the same thing about me! Being transformed into the image of Christ is evidence that there is life in our Christian faith– and also in our marriage.

Not surprisingly, the world doesn't understand this, and therefore there is no forgiveness, no patience, no true tolerance. Children in our current self-centered culture are not seen as a blessing but a curse. The right of the mother to kill her offspring dominates, and perversion of marriage relationships seeks to redefine the very meaning of love as

God has established it. Instead, we live in a world of selfishness, accusations, anger, and confrontation. Without the transforming power of Christ, there is only death.

A strange thing is happening in our current culture as this is being written. There is a rising tide of gross (or even in some cases, of insignificant, or even fabricated) accusations being dug up– particularly from those who hold public office– against others for transgressions that allegedly took place far in the past. There's an assumption that the accused cannot change, that they must be judged according to actions they committed 30 years ago or according to actions that a particular race committed generations ago, and therefore they are not qualified to run for public office. What a dark and sad world it is when there is no transformation.

The world cannot comprehend the reality that through repentance, transgressions can be forgiven through faith in Jesus Christ who already bore our sins to pay the penalty for them. Consequently, without the grace of God, this problem is snowballing as the accused retaliate by digging up offenses in kind, perpetuating a culture marked with blaming others, and creating a world of suspicion, anger, and fear.

Christians, on the other hand, understand that there is *no one* who is innocent of past transgressions. NO one. Romans 3:23 is a constant reminder that, "*all* have sinned and fall short of the glory of God." This pattern of accusation will eventually implode because according to its own standard, every individual will be found guilty. There is not one person apart from Jesus who has a flawless past, who has not sinned.

Those who are **in Christ** have a completely different view than the world does. We live our lives in constant humility before God, exercising daily repentance for sins we commit. When we repent of our sins, we have the assurance that they are forgiven through the shed blood of Christ- true reconciliation. We are brought out of the darkness of our sin, and transformed by the life of Christ in us. Once, we were children of darkness but now we are children of light. We know that we are all in the growing process of transformation. We are not yet what we will be, but thank God, we are not what we used to be.

I cringe at the immaturity and thoughtlessness of many of my actions when I was a teenager or even a young bride. But I've been forgiven, and instead, I choose to consider those transgressions as signposts of Christ's forgiveness extended to me, the markers of how much He has changed me since then. Frankly, I cringe at the mistakes and immaturity I see in myself even now! And yet I know I am still in the process of being changed into His image, and I need to walk a life marked with repentance. I am not yet what I will be when I am fully formed. When I am, I will look like Him and I will see Him face to face.

We are not like the world. We are forgiven for the past sins that we have repented of, and we can forgive others who are also in the process of being changed into the image of Christ for their past sins that Christ has forgiven.

Romans 12:2 urges us to carefully avoid the ungodly patterns that the world demonstrates,

> "Do not be conformed to this world, but be transformed by the renewal of your mind, that by testing you may discern what is the will of God, what is good and acceptable and perfect."

Nothing on this earth can be so wonderful. Thanks be to God that by the life of Christ that flows in us as we live in Him, we are being changed into His glorious image.

CHAPTER 9

Formed in Darkness, Glimpses of Light

Imagine– or maybe remember– that heart-wrenching, startled expression on a newborn's face as he leaves the darkness of the womb and is forcibly pushed into the intense brightness of light. His eyes squint, his face scowls, and he immediately lets out a heartrending cry of bewilderment at the stark, overwhelming change. What a mind-boggling contrast!

There can't possibly be a better way to describe the jolting change that we undergo when we are born again than by the explosive contrast between darkness and light.

> "At one time, you were darkness, but now you are light in the Lord. Walk as children of light," (Ephesians 5:8).

For the last nine months of his life, the baby has been shaped and formed within the dark confines of the womb. All he has ever known is darkness. It was in the darkness that he was prepared in every way for the moment when he would be brought into amazing light. Psalm 139 is David's song of praise over the miraculous way in which he, like this little baby, was "made in secret, intricately woven in the depths of the earth."

And yet in that very same chapter, just prior to David's exultation over how he was miraculously formed in the darkness of the womb, he tells the almost incomprehensible fact that darkness– no matter how intense– can never overcome God. It's God Who overcomes the darkness.

In his overwhelming revelation as he pondered this, David sang a psalm,

> "If I say, 'Surely the darkness shall cover me, and the light about me be night,' even the dark is not dark to You; the night is bright as the day, for darkness is as light with you," (Ps.139:11,12).

Let's think for a minute about the incredible reality of what this means.

Here we are, in the darkness of the world, surrounded by sin on every side. Can it really be true that God is not rattled by the darkness that confounds us in this world, in this "womb of heaven?" When we get to heaven, we will enter unimaginable brightness when we come into the physical presence of God; but right now, just like the child being formed in the darkness of the womb, we are also being shaped and formed in a very dark place. And yet God is not at all confounded by the darkness– it's His workshop.

There's absolutely no doubt about it: the world as we know it is a very dark place. Sometimes it really feels like evil is dominating, and we can understandably become worn out and discouraged, overwhelmed by the sweeping wickedness. And yet this is the very place that God has chosen to form us into His image.

From the time that Adam sinned, the world has been a dark place. Even as Jesus ascended back into heaven, He left His disciples in a world that was still filled with sin. Though the light Himself had come into that darkness, the darkness could not even comprehend it, (John 1:5). The children of darkness were blind. And yet even in that very darkness, those who were the children of light saw light- the light that shone in the midst of the darkness.

Here in the world, we are surrounded by darkness, but believe it or not, the darkness cannot overcome us. God has promised to be with us even when we're surrounded by utter darkness.

In 1834, Edward Mote was convinced of this reality when he wrote in a hymn:

> "When darkness seems to hide His face, I rest in His unchanging grace..."[23]

What incomprehensible peace we have so that we can 'rest,' even when we're surrounded by the darkness of sin. We rest in Him. The world cannot understand this because it defines 'peace' according to circumstances– according to what's external. The world believes that if circumstances can just be changed or manipulated, then it will bring peace. But it never lasts because circumstances are unstable, always changing.

---

[23] Edward Mote, *circa* 1834; first appeared in *Mote's Hymns of Praise*, 1836. Originally titled "The Immutable Basis of a Sinner's Hope," various changes in the lyrics have evolved over time, including this phrase which originally was, 'When darkness veils his lovely face." I have chosen to use this accepted change because of the clarity of the fact that darkness merely *seems* to hide his face.

God never changes. He doesn't define peace according to circumstances– but according to His light. If His light is in us, even in the worst of circumstances there is peace.

It's fascinating to realize that a developing baby at only 16 weeks gestation can perceive light, even as he's in the darkness of the womb; and by 22 weeks he might kick or wiggle in response to flashing light on mom's belly. If there is life, there is the perception of light, even in a dark place. And yet prior to birth, a developing baby cannot bear the intensity of full light yet.

Repeatedly, God is described in the Bible as light. Right now, if we were exposed to the fullness of His light while we're still here in the womb of heaven, not yet fully formed, we would not be able to endure it. In Exodus 33 and 34, Moses asked God to show him His glory, but God told him that he did not have the human capacity to bear it, because man could not see such brightness and live. He covered Moses with His hand and let him see only His back, and still, Moses' exposure to the intense light of God left his own face glowing with such brilliance that it was necessary for him to wear a veil when he spoke to the Israelites. They couldn't bear even the reflection of God's great light.

Sin simply cannot stand in the brightness and glory of God's presence. His light is like the consuming fire that Hebrews 12:29 and Malachi 3:2 tell us about- it literally consumes sin in us. God is that light.

Earlier, God had first apprehended Moses' attention in the wilderness in the form of a bush aflame with fire, and yet the bush itself was not consumed (Exodus 3). When God spoke from it, Moses hid his face because he was afraid to look at the light of God's presence (v.6). That's the inevitable response when we are confronted with the consuming fire of God's light, because the light of God and the darkness of sin simply cannot coexist.

Is it any wonder that a dark world hates the light of the Christian faith? Light exposing sin produces guilt and shame, and the world can't bear the guilt and shame. The unrepentant seek every way possible to try to appease the unbearable guilt– by changing the rules, laws, and even the very definitions themselves of words like 'love,' or 'marriage' to give license to their sin. When that doesn't take the guilt away, they attempt to force and coerce others around them to not only accept, but to embrace and rejoice in their perversions. And when it all still fails to relieve their guilt, they turn on the Christian faith itself when the light of the Gospel of Christ exposes their sin. Yet there is nothing that can appease guilt and shame, except God Himself– the light– through Christ.

Just as a babe in the womb responds to light revealed in the darkness, God has called us to be the reflection of His light in a very dark world. If there is life, there will be a response to the light. But we shouldn't be surprised when the kingdom of darkness itself doesn't recognize the light, and hates us for not embracing their darkness. They are blind.

God is light. Ezekiel had visions of God and described Him with words like "gleaming metal, sparkling like bronze"; "a bright fire"; "burning coals of fire"; "a flash of lightning"; "a fire infolding itself with brightness all about it."

When he saw a vision of Jesus (that is, "a form that had the appearance of a man," the image of the invisible God) in chapter 8:2, Ezekiel said He had, "the appearance of fire... from his loins upward, the appearance of brightness..." as Jesus exuded the intense brightness of God.

Job described God as "golden splendor"; Isaiah referred to "the brightness of thy rising," and wrote that, "The Lord shall be unto you everlasting light." Later, Isaiah prophesied that, "Gentiles shall come to the light and kings to the brightness of thy rising."

In the New Testament, Mark described the transfiguration of Jesus in 9:2 as being "resplendent with divine brightness." Luke wrote in chapter 9 that Jesus "appeared in splendor and majesty and brightness." Hebrews described Jesus as being "the brightness of [God's] glory."

And, of course, Saul was dramatically apprehended on the road to Damascus by a blinding light that brought about his conversion, as recorded in Acts 9. Not much later, in Acts 12, Peter was released from his prison when a bright light shone in his cell.

In Revelation, John described his vision of Jesus: "He who sat there appeared like the brightness of jasper," and Revelation 21:23 says of the New Heaven and New Earth that, "the city has no need of sun or moon to shine on it, for the glory of God gives it light, and its lamp is the Lamb."

Light is the very character of God. In John 8:12, Jesus said, "I am the light of the world. He that follow me shall not walk in darkness, but shall have the light of life."

We spoke earlier of how Christians have perpetually been wrongly fixated on God's form, and yet what He really desires is for us to know the nature of His light. It's His light that gives meaning to our Christian faith.

C.S.Lewis wrote,

> "I believe in Christianity as I believe that the Sun has risen. Not only because I see it, but because by it I see everything else."[24]

The sun itself is impossible for us to gaze upon, just as the brightness of Christ is impossible for us, in our present form, to gaze upon. But it's the nature of illumination that makes light so deeply compelling. Our faith is not transformed because of the form of God, but because His light is so infinitely revealing.

We are called out of the darkness into His light, even as we are still in the world. Psalm 112:4 reminds us that even in this present evil world, "Light arises in the darkness."

While we're still in the darkness of this world, the light is revealed to us in the measure that God sees fit for us. If the fulness of His light exposed to us all of our sinful condition at

---

[24] C.S. Lewis, *The Weight of Glory,* (New York, NY, Harper Collins Publishers, 1976), 140

once, it would be so overwhelming we would not be able to tolerate it.

Thankfully, like the baby in utero who responds to limited light that shines into his darkness until the full force of bright light surrounds him on his birth, we, too, are led by God's revealed light, just enough to reveal our sin, and to guide us in the way we should go as we're groping around in the darkness of this present world– leading us literally one step at a time. Faith is following the light, one step at a time, even when we are not clearly able to see what's ahead of us.

The book of 1 John is a whole chronicle of living in the light, of being born into the Kingdom of God, and of how we can know that we are in Him. The first chapter begins in verse 5 by affirming that,

> "God is light, and in him is no darkness at all. If we say we have fellowship with him while we walk in darkness, we lie and do not practice the truth.
>
> But if we walk in the light, as he is in the light, we have fellowship with one another, and the blood of Jesus his Son cleanses us from all sin."

The blindness of sin is what creates darkness, and God mercifully opens our blind eyes as we are formed into His image, just as the eyes of the forming baby in utero are gradually opened. Isaiah 42:16 characterizes the nature of His light when God says,

> "I will lead the blind in a way that they do not know, in paths that they have not known, I will guide them. I will turn the darkness before them into light, the rough places into level ground. These are the things I do, and I do not forsake them."

The NASB beautifully translates that last phrase as "...These are the things I will do, and I will not leave them undone."

He is determined to form us into His image as He leads us– by His revealed light– through the darkness of the world. He has not called us out of the world yet, but He has promised to be the light that shines in the darkness as He is actively at work in us.

Stuart Townend, one of the most inspiring songwriters of our day, wrote a wonderful rendition of John Henry Newman's hymn of 1833 that so perfectly conveys this reality:

> "Lead on, lead on O kindly Light
> Amid th'encircling gloom;
> Though far from home in the darkest of night
> Still, You will lead me on.
>
> The distant scene, the path before me
> I do not ask to see
> But guard my feet o'er mountain and valley
> One step sufficient for me..."[25]

We are children of light. Even in darkness, we are guided by the light. The children of darkness can't see it because they are

---

[25] Stuart Townend, Townend Songs, 2017; John Newman, 1833

blind, but to us, it's breathtaking. While we're in His workshop– the womb of heaven– we're growing, being transformed into the image of Christ, changing from one degree of glory to another.

Can we know that we're in the light? Yes, we can! There are clear indications in 1 John, a checklist of the signs of life:

> 1 John 1:7, "If we walk in the light as He is in the light, we have fellowship with one another, and the blood of Jesus cleanses us from all sin."
>
> 1 John 2:3, "By this we know that we have come to know him, if we keep his commandments."
>
> 1 John 2:5, "By this we may know that we are in him... to walk in the same way in which he walked."
>
> 1 John 2:9, "Whoever loves his brother abides in the light."
>
> 1 John 2:15, "If anyone loves the world, the love of the Father is not in him....but whoever does the will of God abides forever."

The children of darkness can see only darkness, which is why their battle cry is for death and barrenness. The world could not comprehend the light when Jesus came right into the midst of darkness, and even today, there are those in the darkness of this world who are blinded by sin, and cannot comprehend light, even when this miracle is right in front of their eyes.

We are His children, His heirs. We're called by God to reflect Him as light in the darkness of the world. Ironically, it's by reflecting His light in a dark place that we ourselves are being formed into the image of God.

> "You are a chosen race, a royal priesthood, a holy nation, a people for His own possession, that you may proclaim the excellencies of Him who called you out of darkness into His marvelous light." (1 Peter 2:9)

CHAPTER 10

In the World, but Not of the World

A picture on Facebook swept over me with a mix of terrible anger and deep sadness. It showed two women, both wearing teeshirts that screamed, "My body, my choice!" At the same time, in a twist to accommodate the now undisputed fact that the baby is not the woman's body, they held signs that claimed, "A parasite doesn't have rights!"

As sad and angry as I was over the careless, irreverent reference to a child made in the image of God, I was likewise incredulous over the irony of blatant contradiction within their own argument. On the one hand, their teeshirts claimed that the growing baby was part of their body, while at the same time, their signs admitted that it was not.

The intense war over the legality of killing pre-born babies has been going on for a long time in our generation. Yet the pro-abortion argument keeps changing, of necessity, to accommodate undeniable facts as they are revealed through technology or reasonable debate– as the photo mentioned above exemplifies. There was a time we remember when it was argued that the growing baby was not considered to be life at all, only a "clump of tissue." But intrauterine photography has proven that wrong, and the reality of a growing child can't be denied anymore.

Then the argument changed a bit to claim that although it's undeniably a baby, the baby isn't viable until he is actually born and breathing. But the evidence of ultrasound has proven viability in the womb, showing the baby's ability to sleep, wake, kick, stretch, respond to music, feel and react to pain, suck his thumb– clear for all to see.

Then the argument changed again to claim that even though this is, in fact, a live baby, it's part of the mother's body, and therefore she has the ultimate choice over whether or not to terminate the life. But the discovery of DNA has proven that the growing child is a completely different body, separate from the mother in which it is growing. It's in her body, but it's not her body.

There's no denial that it's life anymore, and the argument has now turned to the value of the life, and who has the right to kill that life if it isn't deemed valuable enough. If it wasn't planned, it's considered to be an unwanted "parasite"– separate from the mother, but attached to her body. And an unwanted, unplanned "parasite" has no value, and therefore can be easily disposed of, they argue.

By definition, a parasite is "an organism that lives in or on an organism of another species (its host) and benefits by deriving nutrients at the other's expense." The baby that is growing in the womb is clearly the same species as his mother. As in all of God's creation, the young that's growing in its own species is called offspring, not a parasite.

He is in his mother; but he is not his mother. He is like her, but he is not her.

A baby being formed in utero is in the womb, but is not part of the womb. He is in the darkest recesses of his mother's body–but he is not part of her body. A mother cannot kill her child by claiming that it's her body she is making a decision about. That is simply not true.

Both the child's blood and the child's DNA are distinct from the mother, defining him clearly as a separate body from hers, a separate and unique individual of the same species. Even in its earliest form of development, a baby is marked as his very own person, completely different even from his mother. His DNA is similar to his mother's and proves that he is of the same species as she is, and yet its characteristics are different even from hers, separating his individuality from hers.

His blood, too, is often a completely different type than that of his mother, as was the case in each of my own children. I have AB- blood while my children all have B+ (which one of my sons claims is the reason for his optimistic disposition.) As the Rh- factor indicates, my blood has a lack of a protein on the red blood cells known as D antigen, and every time I had a baby or a miscarriage, I was given a shot of RhoGam to neutralize the possibility that my blood had developed antibodies that could potentially destroy the red blood cells in the Rh+ blood of a developing future child. The fact that a mother's blood has the potential of attacking the baby's indicates that they are not the same body, though they are of the same species.

DNA and the child's blood type mark the unique individuality of every single person who has ever existed, from their earliest forms. Every child's particular family traits are identifiable in his DNA, but he is quite literally his own unique person. (We ought to stop here for a minute to try to comprehend the vastness of God's amazing infinite creativity.)

This fact helps us to grasp the reality that as Christians, we are in the world, but not part of the world. Just as the child's months within his mother's womb are temporary, so also our time in the world is just temporary. This is one of the most baffling concepts for us to grasp, and yet it's vital that we do.

In Jesus' prayer for his disciples in John 17, he said in verses 15 and 16,

> "I do not ask that you take them out of the world, but that you keep them from the evil one. They are not of the world, just as I am not of the world."

Though Jesus' disciples were in the world, they were different from the world; and Jesus had no intention of snatching them out of it until they were fully formed. Those who were expecting the coming of the Messiah thought that when He came, He would change the world. They thought a Messiah would change their circumstances. They expected Him to remove the bondage, the hurt, the sin, the evil, the sadness, the discouragement, the heavy labor. But He didn't.

His work and His purpose were internal, not external. Instead, He changed hearts so that those who believed in Him would find life. In Him, they would find strength to remain in the world and yet be completely different from it.

As long as we are in the world, we, too, are completely different from it. In the last chapter, we talked about the darkness that characterizes the world right now– the "womb of heaven." When Jesus ascended into heaven, He left His disciples in darkness, and yet those who were His were set apart from the darkness of their environment. After He was resurrected and ascended into heaven, the Holy Spirit came to reside within His followers, equipping them to grow and thrive, even in the darkness.

This Kingdom that we are a part of– the Kingdom of God– looks so different from the world. It speaks differently than the world does. It behaves differently. Its goals and its purposes are so different from those of the world. While the world seeks to compete against and tear down others, we are committed to seeing godly success in each other, even when it means confronting sin that seems painful for the moment.

Right now, the world is characterized by death and barrenness. What amazing joy that we are characterized by life and fruitfulness!

The world worships man; we worship the one true God. The world seeks accolades and satisfaction in pleasing self; we find our joy is pleasing God. The world tries to manipulate and change identity; we rejoice in the security of who we are in Christ. The world strives for control and the manipulation of others; we submit to Jesus Christ as the supreme authority over all.

Romans 12:9-21 gives us the character that defines what we ought to look like that stands in stark contrast to the world we are in– as different as light is from darkness.

> "Let love be genuine. Abhor what is evil; hold fast to what is good. Love one another; outdo one another in showing honor; be fervent in spirit, serve the Lord; rejoice in hope, be patient in tribulation, be constant in prayer; contribute to the needs of the saints, show hospitality;
>
> "Bless those who persecute you; rejoice with those who rejoice, weep with those who weep; Live in harmony; do not be haughty; do not be wise in your own eyes; repay no one evil, live peaceably with all...
>
> "Do not be overcome by evil, but overcome evil with good."

As Christians who are active, thriving members of the Body of Christ, we the Church maintain a "counter- culture" in this present world that sets us apart– in stark contrast– from the world. In John 13, Jesus gave instruction to His followers.

> "A new commandment I give to you, that you love one another: just as I have loved you, you also are to love one another," He said. "By this all people will know that you are my disciples, if you have love for one another."

God has given us His instruction manual in order for us to work out this godly love toward our fellow man. It's important to be reminded that love, whether it's toward a husband, wife, child, or fellow Christian, is not merely an expression of emotion but an act of care and protection toward each other.

In his book Mere Christianity, C.S.Lewis defined the true meaning of love as it related to a husband and wife, but his wisdom applies very well to others in the family of God:

> "Being in love is not merely a feeling, but a deep unity, maintained by the will, and deliberately strengthened by habit, reinforced by the grace which both partners ask and receive from God."[26]

And so it is. That's the character of love that sets us apart from the world. We define love as the Bible defines it. Again, Romans 12:9 defines what love really is. "Let love be genuine. Abhor what is evil; hold fast to what is good." Our concept of words is not like the world's. We are in the world, but we are not like the world. Inevitably, we will look different than the world.

Right now, there's an intense cultural war going on all around us, a persistent attack against Christian faith by humanists claiming that man is God. The philosophy is as ludicrous as assuming the child in utero is his mother, able to think, act, or make the decisions as a mother. The deceptive philosophy of humanism– the worship of man instead of God– seeks to

---

26 C.S.Lewis, *Mere Christianity,* (San Francisco, Harper Collins Publishers, 1952) 109

claim ultimate authority over every area of life, assuming the role of God, assuming that man is God. But man is not God.

Eventually, a baby may look very much like his mother. But he is not his mother. He is in her, but he is not her. As believers in Christ, we are in God, but we are not God. And yet as we abide in Him, we are growing more and more like Him.

> "...What partnership has righteousness with lawlessness? Or what fellowship has light with darkness?...Therefore go out from their midst and be separate from them, says the Lord...and I will be a father to you, and you shall be sons and daughters to me, says the Lord Almighty," (2 Corinthians 6:14-18).

CHAPTER 11

His Word is Our Food

An early snowstorm hit with a vengeance in upstate New York when my first child was born, creating a bitterly cold late November. In that unique place, blinding snow is driven across the Great Lakes, producing unbelievable blizzard conditions. When we brought our baby home from the hospital in it, the harsh chill seemed to underscore the reality of my responsibility as it hit hard.

The overworked furnace had shut down by the time we got home, and in the freezing apartment, I collapsed into an armchair and cried hard, overwhelmed with ***both*** intense joy and intense responsibility, feeling the heavy weight of my inability. The joyful elation of having given birth to our new baby was still there– but it was mixed with a rush of reality over the responsibility we had just begun to bear. And yet I knew I wouldn't give it up for anything in the world.

The new responsibilities, new chores, new routines, new realities, even the constant interruptions all very soon became a normal definition of my life that I thrived in. And yet a quiet, underlying sense of responsibility in raising children never left me. Raising our children was the very happiest chapter of my life, and yet at the same time, it was the most intense, sober one I've ever known.

Had I been negligent in my responsibilities, it wouldn't have changed the fact that I was a mother– but it would have shaped my role as one.

Our birth into the Kingdom of God is just like that. The great joy of rebirth is far deeper than anything we have ever known, and goes beyond any sense of 'happiness' that's merely superficial. Yet it's set apart from anything else we've ever known because it's tightly interwoven–ironically– with responsibility.

We're called *up* into greater things through the responsibility He gives to us in our new birth. We are saved by His grace alone. Our obedience to His instructions, His Law– His Word to us– isn't what makes us part of His family, but it's what shapes us once we are.

The incredible joy over sins– *my* sins– that are forever forgiven, and the wonderful reality of being born into this amazing Kingdom is truly overwhelming, in such a good way. At the same time, responsibility is a constant underlying companion of our joy. We are called to reflect the beauty of God by carrying the responsibilities of being members of such an honorable family. Our obedience, or neglect of it, doesn't change our identity as sons of God, but it defines the character of what He wants us to be as His children. What a privilege!

God's Word is the nourishment by which we grow. Even during the baby's nine months in utero, he grows and is transformed as he receives nourishment from the placenta through the umbilical cord. If the nutrition– his food– were to be cut off, he would die. A baby in utero cannot be sustained without nourishment. Likewise we, in the womb of heaven, must be nourished continually by God's Word in order to thrive. We simply cannot grow or remain healthy if we are not feeding on His Word, our spiritual food.

God's instructions for life and living are for our good and for His glory as He is reflected in us. His commands become a normal, easy, truly enjoyable part of how we live our lives as we are in His family. (Okay, I hear you. Sometimes it isn't joyful and sometimes it sure isn't easy. But we obey because we love Him and our all-consuming desire is to please the Father.)

What parents would refuse to have rules and instruction for their children? Only negligent ones. A mother's instruction– her "word"– is in her child's best interest and for his protection. It's the wisdom by which he will thrive as he grows; likewise, God's instructions are for our good and our protection.

There is always a perpetual sense of responsibility that we carry as children of God because the deepest desire of our hearts is to please our Father and reflect His Kingdom on the earth as we obey Him. We want to grow in Him and ultimately look like Him. His Word guides us in how to do it.

Psalm 119, as lengthy as it is (176 verses!) is David's enthusiastic repetition of how much he loves God's Law– God's instruction manual– and finds his greatest delight in His precepts; His rules; His statues; His commandments; His Word; His promise; His judgments; His testimonies.

He sang, "Great peace have they who love Your Law;" "Your statutes have been my songs;" "Oh how I love Your law!" (So when is the last time your kids swooned like that over your rules?)

One of the most damaging missteps the church at large has taken in this last generation has been the disregard of God's Law as relevant to New Testament believers. In truth, when God created all things, He gave us the "instruction manual" to guarantee the success of men and nations. Whenever any culture believes that God's Laws are archaic, and that his own man-made laws are superior to God's, he reaps the "curses" that we are warned will inevitably result when we step outside of His protective, directive Law. We are currently witnessing the unintelligible chaos that always results when man usurps God's Law, as has been the case all throughout history. At the same time, it amazes me how relevant the Laws of God are even now, in our current modern times.

As we saw in a previous chapter, observers– even close ones– can only perceive the seemingly restrictive cost that believers appear to pay. To those who have never experienced new birth themselves, our obedience to God's Law appears to be nothing more than painful legalism; unyielding submission to commands that restrict and prohibit what they perceive as freedom. And yet to those who have truly experienced new birth, there's an ecstasy that's worth it all because we know it's for our good, our protection, and even more, for God's glory. It leads us to *true* freedom, to *true* love, to *true* understanding.

> "Everyone who believes that Jesus is the Christ has been born of God, and everyone who loves the Father loves whoever has been born of him. By this we know that we love the children of God, when we love God and obey his commandments... and his commandments are not burdensome," it says in 1 John 5:1-3.

God's Word is more than merely a responsibility to us, though it is a responsibility. The care I exercised toward my child was a responsibility– and yet I *loved* it. At the same time, my baby's ability to eat, to exercise, and to obey my commands were his delight. My commands were not burdensome; they were the means by which he thrived. God's Law is our protection, given to us in order that we would thrive in life and fruitfulness.

To those of us who are born into His Kingdom, God's Law (or as David sang, His Word; His commandments; His instruction to us) is our daily food. It's pretty instinctive when we're born again, really, to be hungry for our spiritual food. I remember it well. I remember devouring my Bible when I was born again. What had seemed dry and meaningless before was now making complete sense, and feeding me.

Upon birth, the baby's instinct is to cry out so that air can fill his lungs, and instinctively, he gobbles the milk that's ingeniously provided for him. That's exactly what happens to us when we are born into His Kingdom. An inevitable hunger for God's Word to feed us arises when we are truly born again. When anyone suggests that God can better be found while riding a horse or hiking in the mountains than in His written Word, that individual is suggesting an attractive feel-good substitute, but not faith in the one true God. They have not experienced being born again.

With this in mind, 1 Peter 2:2 urges us:

> "Like newborn infants, long for the pure spiritual milk, that by it you may grow up into salvation– if indeed you have tasted that the Lord is good."

We saw that hunger in David. We recognized that hunger in ourselves. It's the inevitable result of those who are truly born again– who have *experienced* new birth, not just observed it.

Unless we experience new birth for ourselves, it's impossible to really know this love for God's Word– the food that sustains us in our indescribable joy over the forgiveness of our sins and birth into the Kingdom of Heaven. His Law is the instruction manual of how we must live life in the Kingdom into which we have been born. This is the truest reality we will ever know, and as King David sang, it is truly our delight.

> "If your law had not been my delight, I would have perished in my affliction. I will never forget your precepts, for by them you have given me life." (Psalm 119:92, 93)

CHAPTER 12

The Heartache of Barrenness

There's a tiny ancient hilltop city in Tuscany that sits at the top of a pinnacle. It's stunningly beautiful. Because of its position, there's only one way to get there– by walking up a very long, steep pedestrian bridge that goes straight up. It's a hard climb, becoming harder the older I get. But there is no other way to enter the city except that one way.

This past year my husband and I returned for the third time to this hilltop city called Civita di Bagnoregio. I love this place, and my anticipation was high– and yet this time the experience that I thought would be so thrilling left me feeling rather deflated. A few days prior, I'd been hit with severe asthma, and felt exhausted and weak. On top of that, tourists had overrun the place in such a way that the magic and the thrill were gone for me. The friends we'd brought with us had a wonderful time, of course, mesmerized by their experience in the place, but I couldn't shake off my disappointment. It just wasn't what I had hoped it would be.

I think of this hilltop city when I consider the fact that there is only one way for us– every one of us– to get to this planet: through birth. There is no other way. We all come in exactly the same way, and yet once we've arrived, no two people have ever had the same experience in it.

There's no question that life on this earth is full of beauty and truly wonderful experiences. Once we arrive here, all of us head out of the gate with such enthusiasm, and far too often with unrealistic expectations of what it should bring. It's true, life brings some awesome opportunities; and yet often enough, we're really let down when it does not turn out to be what we thought it would be.

Things that ought to be a normal, easy part of life sometimes become an unreachable, illusive dream that never seems to find fulfillment.

Conception is sometimes one of those things.

Unless a woman has known for herself the emptiness of being barren when she has yearned for children, it's impossible to comprehend the depth of such an unfulfilled hope. Proverbs 30:15 and 16 tries to grasp the devastation by listing it among these heartbreaking issues:

> "...Sheol, the barren womb, the land never satisfied with water, and the fire that never says, 'Enough!'"

The very definition of the word –"bleak and lifeless"– expresses the depths of emptiness that barrenness represents. Stories of barren women in the Bible express the grief that each of them bore. Genesis 11 tells about Sarai and her frustration– and eventual efforts to try to make it happen by herself– over not being able to conceive.

Genesis 25 tells of Isaac who prayed to the Lord on behalf of his wife Rebekah because she was barren. Genesis 29 and 30 tell of Rachel's barrenness, and Judges 13 tells of Manoah's wife who couldn't conceive. In 1 Samuel 1, Hannah wept and refused to even eat because of her grief, and when Eli observed her distress, he misinterpreted it as drunkenness. Then Luke tells of Elizabeth's inability to conceive.

Ruth's indirect story of barrenness had to do with shattered dreams. A Moabite, she had married an immigrant from Bethlehem of Judah. Ruth obviously loved her husband because she was deeply grieved when he died at a young age, before he was able to give her children. With the shattered pieces of her life, she chose to move to a new country with her mother-in-law, perhaps running from her grief, disappointment, and her devastation.

But there, Ruth's story took a huge change. Where she had previously married a young husband with the hope of having children with him, after he died she found herself married to a much older man– her late husband's close relative– who was assigned to her through the Jewish levirate law, a law of the new country to which she had just immigrated.

All the stories of these women were recorded because every one of them eventually conceived and bore a child whom God used in a very significant role in order to bring about His purposes– in Ruth's case, the son who was the lineage that Jesus Himself would come from.

To read these accounts seems to give assurance that God was obviously in control, waiting for "the fullness of time" to bring His plans into play. But is God's perfect plan always conception?

Can it be that barrenness itself is sometimes His perfect plan?

The woman longing for a child might wonder if the inability to conceive was a reflection of God's punishment, as it was in Michal's case in 2 Samuel 6:23. The grieving woman might find herself searching her heart and crying out to God - and yet she knows that her inability to conceive is not God's punishment.

Where are the recorded stories about the faithful, God-fearing women who were never able to conceive at all? Did God's perfect plan come into play in those too, even when there was no sin that should deter it?

It's in the most incomprehensible adversities of life like these that we question whether or not it's true that God is still in control. We question if there really is no random detail in our lives when we are in Christ, and truthfully, it frustrates us to know that there are some questions we may never find answers to, at least while we're still on this earth. To trust Him means that we don't need to know the answers, as hard as that is. He is God and sometimes we will simply never know the reasons why He does what He does.

Always, He maintains sovereign control over every detail of our lives as we live in Him, and ironically, He often uses our harshest disappointments and adversities to reflect the burden of His Kingdom and the deep longing of His own heart. Sarai's attempt to try to bring about God's promise through her own efforts became the picture that points us to the "two covenants" expressed in Galatians 4:21-26: one of the flesh, and the other, the true promise of the Kingdom of God.

Maybe we've been too harsh in our judgment of Sarai, a grieving barren woman. Most likely, her act of giving her servant to her husband was not necessarily one of blatant manipulation as we too often assume it was, but more likely a reflection of her submissive response to the only thing she knew as humanly possible within the culture of her day. She undoubtedly believed God's promise to her husband Abram– but not necessarily to her, considering the obvious reality that she was beyond child-bearing. Giving her servant Hagar to him– which was a cultural practice of the day– was likely her humble submission to what she assumed was a requirement from God Himself in order to fulfill His promise to Abram.

Explaining this in the later context of the prevalent 'anthropomorphism' of Paul's day, R.J.Rushdoony wrote,

> "In Galatians 4:27, [Paul] cites Isaiah 54:1, a statement which defies the humanistic order. The barren woman will have more children than the fruitful wife. The true believer and the true church may seem barren, but to them the Lord gives the great increase. Isaiah refers to Sarai's long barrenness and sees it as revelatory of God's sovereign over-ruling of man's plans in history and in terms of His purposes." [27]

Even Sarai's attempt to participate in bringing about God's plan became part of God's revelation to us.

---

[27] R.J.Rushdoony, *[Commentary on] Romans and Galatians*, (Vallecito, CA, Ross House Publishers, 1997) 383

Right now, there are many women who have been unable to conceive for various reasons– or, much to their great frustration, for no apparent reason. When the crushing grief of barrenness engulfs a woman, it's a very lonely place with a terrible feeling of having been forgotten, and a constant looming self-doubt, wondering, "What did I do to deserve this?"

It's hard to imagine that God Himself could possibly know such grief and carry such sorrow in a meaningful way– but He does. This is exactly the grief He has carried over those who are never born into His Kingdom.

Isaiah 49:14,15 expressed God's intense love for His people – like these barren women– who felt forgotten.

> "Zion said,'The Lord has forsaken me; my Lord has forgotten me.' [And He replies:] 'Can a woman forget her nursing child, that she should have no compassion on the son of her womb? Even these may forget, yet I will not forget you. Behold, I have engraved you on the palms of my hands; your walls are continually before me.'"

The grieving barren are not forgotten. Though they may never give birth, they are the very expression of His own heart revealed to His people. God hears the cries of these women, and the holy longing they express is itself used by God as a prophetic exultation of His greater promise fulfilled through Christ Himself:

> “Sing, oh barren one who did not bear; break forth into singing and cry aloud, you who have not been in labor! For the children of the desolate one will be more than of her who is married, says the Lord,” (Isaiah 54:1, quoted later in Galatians 4:27.)

And yet women longing to be mothers find little comfort in this particular call of God on their lives.

Knowing that God cares, and that He is revealing the cry of His own heart through the physical barrenness of women is small comfort to the childless woman in her deep disappointment. But that’s exactly the point! Sometimes the burdens we carry are relentless and painful, and that’s exactly the way God intended them to be, that His glory would be revealed through our grief.

As American Christians, we so easily fall prey to a preconceived chipper idea of what “the call of God on your life” might mean. Immediately, we think in terms of God having a wonderful plan for your life that’s going to be awesome and you’ll recognize it because it will be so satisfying! Far too many think of the call of God on their lives as having to do only with the church– apostles, prophets, pastors, evangelists, missionaries. To some, the call of God might mean the gift of public speaking and giving great encouragement; for others, it might mean excelling as a successful writer or artist or teacher or designer or business person. We think of “the call of God” as exercising our gifts and talents– musically, professionally, administratively, creatively.

Understandably, we often think of motherhood as being the call of God on our lives, and we immediately equate it with being wonderful and fulfilling, which it is. And yet truth be told, as long as we're in this world, motherhood inevitably carries some grief. Just look around, and you'll see that there are some very disappointed mothers who have struggled with seriously rebellious children. Some with severely disabled children. Some with autistic children. Or no children. It isn't always such a glorious expectation, is it?

There are some parents I've known whose greatest impact has been evident in the amazing examples of true faith they've demonstrated to the church by the way in which they have humbly lived out the heartache of their rebellious children in a God-glorifying way.

Truthfully, the call of God on one's life often involves suffering, though we don't like to hear that.

Mary, the mother of Jesus, is an example of a woman who fulfilled the call of God on her life. For the most part, we think of the indescribable joy it had to have been for Mary to not only be a mother, but to be the mother of the Son of God. I can't even imagine what it must have felt like to be chosen by God for such a calling. What an incomprehensible blessing!

Or was it?

Luke 2:22-38 tells the story of Mary and Joseph taking Jesus to the temple to consecrate him as the firstborn male who opened her womb, in compliance with the command of Exodus 13:1. An old man named Simeon was in the temple at the same time, and began to prophesy about who this child would be. Within the context of his great exaltation, almost as an aside– merely noted within brackets in verse 35 of my Bible– Simeon quickly mentioned to Mary what the call of God on her life would be. Oh, and by the way, Mary, "...a sword will pierce through your own soul also."

What must Mary have thought when he said that? We so easily embrace the glorious part of Mary's call, but there are very few of us who could have embraced the great burden, the deep sadness and incomprehensible grief that Mary was called by God to carry as she watched her son Jesus suffer as He did.

We have to understand this. Sometimes the call of God on a woman's life is carried through by way of suffering and grief in order to fulfill His plan and His purpose, and reveal His Kingdom. Through the deep and sincere longing of a woman's heart for motherhood, we understand God more. We identify with Him in a greater way.

Life has deep losses, and they are all part of our transformation into becoming more like Christ. Many years ago, I sat alone on the porch of my house in a daze of deep grief over a lost friendship through very difficult circumstances. I felt so devastated, I couldn't speak or even pray. In my terrible sorrow, the words of Isaiah 53 came into my mind suddenly, with boldness and clarity: "He was despised and rejected by men; a man of sorrows, and acquainted with grief, and as one from whom men hide their faces he was despised, and we esteemed him not. Surely he has borne our griefs and carried our sorrows…"

Never before that moment had I understood how much Jesus identified with my deepest griefs in a very true way. But even more than that, I realized that in my own grief of rejection, I had been given a gift of identifying with Him in His sorrow.

It takes very little faith to identify with Him in the greatness and power of His resurrection life; but we won't really know Him fully unless we also identify with His suffering. Paul wrote in Philippians 3:8-10:

> "For his sake I have suffered the loss of all things…that I may gain Christ and be found in him…that I may know him and the power of his resurrection, and may share his sufferings, becoming made like him."

We can merely survive the grief and pain of adversity– in this case, of barrenness– or we can be faithful stewards of it, reflecting Christ. We will all be called by God, at some points, to suffer painful circumstances because we cannot really know Jesus unless we share in His suffering by knowing the pain of adversity, as well as His resurrection life.

Barrenness is painful. Let's not try to pretend it isn't. And yet through it, we become more like Christ as we identify with Him in His suffering. Knowing this won't take the pain away, but it strengthens our faith to know that He hears and understands, even when we don't. Realizing that our barrenness enlarges our capacity for Him as we identify with

Him transforms the pain and grief, even if it doesn't take the grief and pain away.

And often, it's the pain of barrenness that leads right into God's intentional fulfillment in another remarkable picture of our entrance into the Kingdom of Heaven– understanding our adoption as sons. In a very real way, barrenness itself can become the means by which God reveals our entrance into His Kingdom, His family– a wonderful reality of the beauty that comes from ashes.

> "Sing, o barren one... Break forth into singing...Enlarge the place of your tent and let the curtains of your habitations be stretched out; do not hold back; lengthen your cords and strengthen your stakes, for you will spread abroad to the right and to the left..." (Isaiah 54:1,2)

CHAPTER 13
Adopted

On a warm summer evening in the Pacific Northwest, my husband and I had the great privilege of meeting a young Ukrainian man, Ruslan Malicuta and his wife Anya who founded an organization called World Without Orphans.

As they were traveling through America sharing their vision, they spent some time in our town, so I prepared a very homey Ukrainian dinner for them– cabbage rolls, pierogies, lots of sour cream and dill. We sat around the large table under the trees in our backyard while their young sons who spoke no English and our young grandsons who spoke no Ukrainian ran around together, laughing, playing games, and interacting with a fascinating communication without understanding of each other's words.

As the adults lingered around the table with coffee and honey cake, Ruslan shared with us the story of how he had come to build an organization that became so successful that it grew from the original Ukraine Without Orphans into a worldwide mission called World Without Orphans. The spark that started it was when it had occurred to him that there were as many churches in Ukraine as there were orphans. He realized that if just one family in every church would adopt a child, they would obliterate the need for orphanages.

The concept is simple enough. What an impact it would make if at least one family from every church adopted an orphan– a truly fatherless child.

Beauty for ashes is a powerful promise of the Gospel of Christ that is evident in adoption.

Isaiah wrote in chapter 61:

> "The Lord has anointed me to bring good news to the poor; he has sent me to bind up the brokenhearted, to proclaim liberty to the captives, and the opening of the prison to those who are bound... to comfort all who mourn... to give them a beautiful headdress instead of ashes, the oil of gladness instead of mourning, the garment of praise instead of a faint spirit...that He may be glorified."

Adoption, like birth itself, is an intentional image of the true reality– and it's such an exact image. Those who were alone, rejected, destitute, and without hope have been brought into the family, provided for, loved, given a name, an identity, and an inheritance.

The Bible tells stories of adoption that, like those of barren women, reveal a very intentional plan of God in order to bring about His Kingdom and the promised Messiah whose coming was foretold. There aren't too many stories of adoption, and yet it's a biblical command to us that's repeated. Pharaoh's daughter adopted Moses, setting the stage for God to use him to bring the deliverance of the Israelites which in turn is a picture of the true reality– our deliverance from the slavery of sin. Eli adopted Samuel. Esther was adopted by her cousin who providentially guided her to deliver the Jews from certain death. And, of course, Jesus was adopted by Joseph.

Adoption carries the great affirmation of being chosen by God.

> "In love he predestined us for adoption as sons through Jesus Christ," Ephesians 1:5 says, "according to the purpose of His will, to the praise of his glorious grace."

The Old Testament chronicles the constant struggle for Jesus' biological family– the Children of Israel– to keep His Law, until Jesus Himself came. When He came to earth, Jesus did not take away the Law, which would only have been an external remedy that wouldn't have changed lives. Instead, He came to change hearts– to change His people internally– in order to provide a way for both Jew and Gentile to be forgiven for breaking His Law, as we all have, through Christ who paid the penalty for us- both the biological and the adopted– who repent and believe in Him.

Jesus provided the way for both Jew and now also the Gentile to find forgiveness. Because of Jesus' death on our behalf, the Gentiles are now those who have been adopted into His family through faith. At that powerful moment of Jesus' death as He paid the price of our sin, the veil of the temple was torn, opening the way into His presence for both Jew and Gentile who through faith in Christ are brought into His family. We– the Gentiles– have been adopted into His family through faith in Christ Jesus.

> "Remember [Gentiles] that you were at that time separated from Christ, alienated from the commonwealth of Israel and strangers to the covenants of promise, having no hope and without God in the world. But now in Christ Jesus you who once were far off have been brought near by the blood of Christ. For he himself...has made us both one and has broken down in his flesh the dividing wall...that he might create one new man instead of two [i.e.Jew and Gentile]...and might reconcile us both to God in one body..." says Ephesians 2:11-22.

As adopted sons of God, we share in every part of His inheritance! Unfaithful biological sons won't have part in the inheritance, but as adopted sons, we have every benefit as legitimate children.

To help us understand, Romans 11:17-24 uses the illustration of unfruitful biological branches being cut off from the olive tree, while other "wild" branches are grafted in to the olive tree, sharing in the nourishing life of the source. That's the beautiful story of adoption. We cannot come into God's Kingdom through DNA, but through faith in Christ's life-giving atoning sacrifice– through adoption.

In a very real way, we were destitute slaves to sin when He delivered us from our former bondage and brought us into His family.

> "For all who are led by the Spirit of God are sons of God. For you did not receive the spirit of slavery to fall back into fear, but you have received the Spirit of

> adoption as sons, by whom we cry, 'Abba! Father!' The Spirit himself bears witness with our spirit that we are the children of God, and if children, then heirs– heirs of God and fellow heirs with Christ, provided we suffer with him in order that we may be glorified with Him," (Romans 8:14-17.)

Through adoption, we who were lost in darkness have been brought into His family, made heirs of the Father. We are forgiven, protected, provided for. We share in the inheritance He has provided, and we now carry His name. Our identity is in Him.

Israel in the Old Testament was the picture pointing to the true reality: the sons of God through faith in Christ Jesus. Adoption today is likewise a necessary and God-inspired picture of our adoption into His family, and the inheritance we have in Christ Jesus.

The greatest words the orphan can hear:

> "I will be a father to you, and you shall be sons and daughters to me," (2 Cor. 6:18.)

And those precious words come from God Himself.

CHAPTER 14

Called to Care for the Destitute

In seven-year-old childish fantasy, I dearly wanted to find out that I had been adopted. As the middle of five consecutive sisters, I longed to be somehow set apart, different, as my only brother who was the eldest was– and adoption seemed like such a romantic idea that fit the narrative. That dream was ridiculously unrealistic, and yet adoption still remains an unrealistic, romantic idea for so many.

Every one of us knows someone who has been adopted. And yet it hasn't always turned out to be a very romantic idea after all, has it? Some adopted children become so absorbed into the fabric of the family, it seems impossible to imagine they were anything but purely biological; yet at the same time, we all know of struggles and heartbreak in families who were almost torn apart because of the adopted child. One mother bemoaned to me regret as she felt like she was stuck with the nasty results of someone else's parental neglect in dealing with her self-centered, angry adopted child. She felt trapped.

With a completely realistic perspective of the joys and heartbreaks of raising children, and yet knowing the certainty of God's heart for adoption as it reflects His Kingdom, Christians must wrestle through understanding our responsibility in caring for the destitute through adoption.

Not just once, but repeatedly, we are commanded in Scripture to care for "the widows, the orphans, and the sojourners [refugees]." These three are grouped together over and over because according to their biblical definitions, these are all characterized by having been left destitute, without provision, without families, and therefore without inheritance.[28]

Alone, all three of these are vulnerable to abuse, and have no protection. The Bible often refers to orphans as "the fatherless," because they are destitute of the provision and protection that fathers are commanded to provide for their children.

Man was created by God to live in relationships, both with God and with our fellow man. Therefore, as members of the family of God, we're commanded to care for these three who are destitute, who have no one to care for, protect, or provide for them; who do not have families to which they belong. The command is not only because it's the kind thing to do, but because it points to the very heart of God Himself and the nature of His Kingdom.

> Deuteronomy 10:18 says, "He executes justice for the fatherless and the widow, and loves the sojourner, giving him food and clothing."
>
> Psalm 68:5 says, "Father of the fatherless and protector of widows is God in his holy habitation. He

---

28 *See Deuteronomy 14:29; 1 Timothy 5:5 among others.

> sets the lonely in families, but the rebellious live in a sun-scorched land."
>
> Zechariah 7:10 says, "Render true judgments, show kindness and mercy to one another, do not oppress the widow, the fatherless, the sojourner, or the poor."
>
> James 1:27 says, "Religion that is pure and undefiled before God the Father is this: to visit orphans and widows in their affliction."

Biblically, the Christian home is the place where responsibility lies to care for the fatherless through adoption; the church is the place commanded by God to care for widows; and both are commanded to care for the refugees-and yet not indiscriminately. While we are commanded to care for the legitimate cases of these three, the Bible also provides protection for both the home and the church from abuse of the evil or ungodly in any of these.

In 1 Timothy 5:3-16, the nature of a true widow is clearly defined, along with warnings of the characteristics of ungodly widows that the church must be on guard against in order to protect itself from abuse. The true widows who are to be cared for are active members of the faith. We can charitably reach out to non-Christians with evangelistic concern, hoping they will come to faith in Christ; but if they are rebellious toward God, we have no biblical obligation to care for them.

Likewise, there are protections and safeguards for the home and church in their responsibility to care for the refugee. As Ruth, a destitute Moabite, was entering the land of Judah to live with her mother-in-law Naomi, the vow she made as a foreigner entering into this new land provided the protective conditions as expressed in Ruth 1:16-17– that is, “your people shall be my people; your God my God.” The levirate law she submitted to in marrying her deceased husband’s near kinsman was a law of this new country to which she had just immigrated. The true refugee cannot come to the new land with the intention of forcing others to submit to his pagan god or to the laws of his previous land.

In his commentary on Exodus, R.J.Rushdoony wrote,

> “Citizenship in the Biblical sense was not and never is a right. It is rather a gift of grace, maintained by law-keeping, and to abuse it is to invite God’s judgement.” [29]

Similarly, adoption is a gift of grace, not a right. The adoptee cannot become part of a home with the intention of living independently of its laws, rules, and Christian faith. If we enter adoption driven purely by emotion instead of the protection of biblical guidance, a multitude of problems will likely arise, as we’ve probably all witnessed in adoptions that have “gone bad.” It isn’t reason enough to adopt merely to satisfy the craving to be a mother, just as it isn’t reason enough to get married for romance alone. Both are life long commitments that will realistically involve rough days as well as good ones.

---

[29] R.J.Rushdoony, *Commentaries on the Pentateuch, Exodus* (Vallecito, CA, Ross House, 2004) p.477

Exodus 22:22 and 23 gives command for mutual protection in the case of adoption, as well as in caring for widows.

> "You shall not mistreat any widow or fatherless child. If you do mistreat them, and they cry out to me, I will surely hear their cry..."

All of God's Law holds the promise of blessings for obedience to Him, and curses for rejecting Him as the Creator and Sustainer who holds ultimate authority. In this particular law, if a widow or orphan is abused and the victim cries out to God, He will hear their cry and bring justice by way of a curse upon the abuser. But it's important to note that God, the Judge and Avenger, brings His righteous acts specifically to those who cry out to Him.

There is mutual protection established here: the vulnerable and destitute are to be protected from abuse, and at the same time, the home and church must be protected from the abuse of the wicked and ungodly. The safety net for the home is ensuring that those who are adopted are submissive participants of the household of faith, who cry out to God in their affliction. As it is in the case of the refugee, the adoptee who comes into the home is also subject to the laws of the home and the God who holds ultimate authority in that home. If he refuses, the home is under no obligation to adopt him.

In his Commentary of Exodus, R.J. Rushdoony noted,

> "There is an important qualification to this judgement in v.23: if 'they cry at all unto me.' God as Judge and

> Avenger acts when there is an appeal unto Him. This qualification places a duty on the covenant community. If they want justice, whatever else they do, they must pray to God. If there is no appeal to Him for His judgement, there is no judgment from Him in these cases. The Supreme Judge acts when His judgment is sought in such matters." [30]

We are commanded to care for and protect those who are afflicted, and yet if any of these three cases of those who are destitute actively blaspheme or rebel against God Himself, then we as His representatives on earth have no obligation to care for them. We cannot participate in enabling those who are against God. Again, R.J.Rushdoony reminded us that,

> "[God's] laws are inescapably concerned with good and evil, and therefore with God– or against Him."[31]

It must be noted that there are many Christian families who have adopted outside of the household of faith, sometimes with much success. The Christian family can exercise a freewill act of charity to adopt, but they are not biblically commanded to do so outside of the faith. Still, the success is predicated upon the adoptee's cooperation with the faith and practices of the home as commanded by God through scripture.

As abortion has become widespread and out of control, the common accusation from liberal pro-abortion individuals

---

30 R.J.Rushdoony, *Commentaries on the Pentateuch, Exodus,* (Vallecito, CA, Ross House Books, 2004) p.319
31 Ibid, p.338.

toward Christians is that we have no right to decry abortion if we aren't willing to adopt all the babies. As Christians, we need to reconcile this. Is it our obligation to adopt all the babies?

Emotionally, we tend to respond to the need wholeheartedly, and yet God's Law is not predicated upon emotion, but on justice. The Christian community ought to adopt the babies rescued from abortion when the mother is confused, raped, or coerced into killing her baby. And yet attempting to adopt the vast number of babies conceived through continuously rebellious anti-Christian lifestyles merely enables sinners to keep on sinning as we snatch up the responsibility they themselves ought to carry, leaving them without consequence. Adopting all the babies does not stop the root of the evil problem of abortion- in a very real way, it just makes it easier.

This current ungodly generation is the clear fruit of the reckless and chaotic thoughts and deeds of individuals who have never had to take responsibility for their own actions but instead coerce others through guilt manipulation into taking the responsibilities they themselves ought to bear. Christians must not feed into it. Removing the consequences of an individual's actions without their repentance merely prevents that sinner from taking responsibility for his/her actions, thereby propagating their sin.

Abortion is murder, not a form of birth control. As Christians, we can never let go of that message or our duty to call those to account who commit murder. And yet at the same time, we must give aid to those who do take responsibility for their actions by helping them in any way we can. Thankfully, there are many excellent pro-life clinics that Christians can participate in– by volunteering, contributing financially, providing supplies, helping to teach young mothers basic infant care– in order to give help and support to mothers who affirm the life of their child.

Christians cannot and must never knowingly enable the propagation of anti-Godly actions, convictions, or beliefs. The biblical command for adoption is first and foremost to the Christian community. The gospels were Holy Spirit inspired written instructions to a persecuted church, in order for the church to create a "counter-culture" against the evil around them- not to absorb the evil culture into their Christian community. Paul encourages us in Galatians 6:10 to

> "do good to everyone, and especially to those who are of the household of faith."

Many times, those who are barren have found fulfillment in adoption; and yet it isn't just the barren who are commanded to adopt. Within the Christian faith, it's all of us who are called by God to care for those without families. Hindered by age or poor health or insufficient finances or extenuating circumstances, we may not all be able to adopt– but we are commanded to find ways to contribute to the cause.

Realistically, for varied reasons, we can't all adopt, but we can all participate in helping those who can. Adoption is expensive. If every family within the church would participate in some way– by donating funds to those who are seeking adoption, by providing clothes and equipment, or by supporting organizations that affirm and assist mothers who choose life over the death of their pre-born child– what a great difference we would make! And in the process of it, we would gain a much greater understanding and appreciation of our own adoption into the Kingdom of Christ.

God's plans are intentional. He has a story that we are so blessed to be part of. Our time on earth is not given for us to merely amuse ourselves or to seek our own earthly happiness until we get to heaven. We are saved for His sake, to participate in the advancement of His Kingdom on the earth. As we do, we are formed more and more into His image.

We are called by God to care for the widows, the orphans, and the destitute. It's far too easy for Christians in the church to sit back comfortably and assume that the government will take care of them– but God has not given this responsibility to civil government. He's given it to you and to me, those of us who profess the name of Christ, that by it, we would better understand Christ and His Kingdom of life and fruitfulness.

Even the most difficult parts of life for us to understand are completely in His sovereign hands, being woven together– in the fullness of time– in such a way that points us consistently to Christ.

Galatians 4:4-7 is the rock that we can rest our confidence upon:

> "When the fullness of time had come God sent forth his Son, born of woman, born under the law, to

redeem those who were under the law so that we might receive adoption as sons.

“And because you are sons, God has sent the Spirit of His Son into our hearts crying, ‘Abba! Father!’ So you are no longer a slave, but a son, and if a son, then an heir through God.”

CHAPTER 15

Blinded by Sin

As a young, busy wife and mother with toddlers scurrying around needing my attention, I was scrubbing the kitchen floor when a great wave of sickness swept over me. Startled, I stopped what I was doing as the reality hit me: I was pregnant again. In that momentary flash, I'm sorry to confess that my initial reaction was something like, "I'm not ready for this! I don't want to be sick like that again right now!"

In all of my pregnancies, the blessing of very fast, uncomplicated deliveries was more than compensated for by severe "morning" sickness that lasted all day long every day for weeks and months on end. Pregnancy for me was defined by constantly dropping whatever I was doing to run to the bathroom and throw up, clean up, and return to the task at hand, always with underlying waves of nausea, like having a case of the flu for several months straight.

From the perspective I have now, I'm ashamed that in the sudden realization that I was growing life– another living soul for the glory of God– I wasn't struck with incredible joy. It's a fact that I'm sad about.

It was only a short matter of time before I felt the awakening of excitement– but I can't take those moments back. I can't erase my bad attitude and replace it with the happiness it deserved. That experience, as quick as it was, revealed to me my own selfish heart, and showed me just how easily we can fall into sin– into self-centeredness, selfish desires, selfish motivations. I saw how vulnerable I was to sin.

How blind we are when we sin. When we let our attention turn, even briefly, from God's great plan and purpose to our own self-serving desires, we become blinded to miracles that are right in front of our eyes. Even when an incredible miracle is held out for us to participate in, instead of beauty and goodness we see only the pain and misery. We only see what it'll cost us, but we shut our eyes tight to the eternal glory of the reward.

Consequently, because sin is so prevalent in our current culture, we find ourselves smack in the middle of a nasty war over who gets to live and who has to die, as mothers bemoan the realization that they are pregnant when they don't want to be. With compelling emotion, pro-abortionists try to convince us (or themselves) that it's really not fair for a child to be born into circumstances that aren't good ones. It's better for them to die. After all, everybody deserves to be wanted. Everyone deserves to have affection. No one should live without having enough food, clothes, a comfortable home, a good education. Right?

Pondering this idea, Dan and I were playing music to work by as we were getting our yard into shape when that old familiar, deep, gravelly voice of Louis Armstrong began to sing out the lyrics of What a Wonderful World. My heart leaped, and I immediately thought, "I love that song!" Isn't that what we wish every child could have? I stopped raking to listen:

"...I see trees of green, red roses too
I watch them bloom for me and you
And I think to myself, What a wonderful world..."[32]

Armstrong's comforting voice sang out about skies of blue, clouds of white, bright blessed days, dark sacred nights, colorful rainbows, friends shaking hands, the love between fellowman. What a wonderful world indeed.

Louis Armstrong sure got it right, didn't he? He understood. In a mere simple song, Armstrong successfully captured the dream that every child deserves.

And yet ironically, it's the very dream that he himself was denied when he was born into this wonderful world he sings about.

Like many up and coming musicians of his day– including Ella Fitzgerald– Louis Armstrong was born in poverty. But unlike many of the rest of them, his poverty was abject. He was born to a prostitute in the lowest, poorest red-light district of New Orleans. Often left to fend for themselves while their mother continued to practice her trade out of desperation to survive in dire times, he and his little sister were frequently left on the streets. With the things we take for granted in life, it's hard to even imagine the degree of neglect in leaving three year old and five year old siblings alone out on the streets of New Orleans.

---

[32] https://www.azlyrics.com/lyrics/louisarmstrong/whatawonderfulworld.html

At the tender age of seven, he found some work with a Russian immigrant family who often let him sleep at their house because there was nowhere else for him to go. It was this Russian family– the Karnofskys– that first recognized musical talent in Louis and got him his first instrument, with which he played music on street corners to earn a few coins for survival.

When he was twelve years old, he was arrested by police for shooting blanks into the air to celebrate New Year's Eve, and was sent to a juvenile detention home for young black boys called The Colored Waifs Home for Boys. But ironically, Louis loved it there. It became the home he'd never had, and the other boys became his family. There was a band at the home that Louis became part of, and his musical talent soared. Though born into desperate conditions we can hardly even imagine, Armstrong pulled himself up out of the mire, and found out that the world really was a wonderful place after all. [33]

Every individual must be given that same chance. The circumstances of an individual's conception or birth do not determine his value, or dictate what he will eventually become. External circumstances are not the definition of a person's worth. In truth, there are very few of us who are born into ideal circumstances. All of us struggle with deficiencies of some sort, many are abused, and all have experienced adversity at some point. Still, every one of us has the inalienable right to life, liberty, and the pursuit of happiness–

---

[33] https://en.wikipedia.org/wiki/Louis_Armstrong

to live in the world God created and experience His providence in it.

If Louis Armstrong had been conceived in today's culture, he would have been at the top of the list of the babies who must be executed, undeserving of life– and of course all the rest of us would have been bereft of the music he gave us, reminding us again that this really is a wonderful world.

Ella Fitzgerald, undoubtedly, would have been on that list too, as well Ringo Starr, Celine Dion, Shania Twain, Johnny Cash, Elvis Presley, Jimi Hendrix, Leonardo DiCaprio... even Oprah Winfrey whose mother was a young, unmarried teenager. According to today's standard of who should live and who should be murdered by abortion, every one of these would have been executed. Meanwhile, the Paris Hiltons of the world, born into every advantage, would be at the top of the list of those most deserving of life.

The worth of a child is not measured by the way in which he was conceived, nor by the circumstances into which he was born. His worth is in the reality that he was created in the image of God, placed on the earth in order to fulfill the purpose for which he was made.

We've been so blinded by sin that we forget that every child is a gift, and every child is created with specific strengths and talents. Every child has the right to find his way in the world– a world of opportunity. What irony that Armstrong ends his beautiful song with the words, "I hear babies cry; I watch them grow. They'll learn much more than I'll ever know. And I say to myself, 'What a wonderful world!'"

So here's the reality check: we've just spent a good amount of time considering the miracle of life, and the most amazing way in which it reflects our birth into the Kingdom of God. And yet God has created this miracle of life in a world that's filled with sinners. Consequently, we will fail sometimes. All of us have sinned and fallen short of the glory of God. But let's never forget that He is a merciful and gracious God Who is so quick to forgive us and restore us. And He redeems even the worst offenses.

Sin so often blinds us so that we don't even recognize that God has given us the great privilege of bringing children into the world, revealing His everlasting Kingdom through the awesomeness of birth. It's such a great privilege that we've been given to lead our children into finding their place in God's Kingdom. There is no a greater joy than knowing that the children you have born walk in Truth.

It's true that sin blinds. But thank God that the light of Christ opens blind eyes and shows us His glory– revealed to us in the birth of a child, just as Jesus Himself came to us. His Kingdom is forever, and it's marked by life and by fruitfulness.

CHAPTER 16

Is Abortion Okay in the Case of Rape?

We live in a fallen world, full of sin. I don't like it. You don't either, but that's the way it is, and that's the way it has always been since Adam was tempted to eat the forbidden fruit "so [he] would be like God" (Genesis 3:5.). Our current culture may seem like the darkest time in history, but it isn't. Ever since sin entered the world, nothing is new, really.

As this is being written, man is again trying to wrestle authority from God because man wants to be God. Right now, there is all out war being played out in our culture against God in a futile attempt to usurp ultimate authority over Him. Again, this is nothing new.

In what was probably the most historic U.S. election ever, there are still many who think the primary conflict in 2020 and 2021 was merely a contentious contest between two presidential candidates. But it wasn't. In truth, this has been a desperate war of two conflicting world-views; of two opposite philosophies of government. It's a war of humanism (the belief that man rules) against the Christian faith (the belief that God rules over all, and man is subservient to Him.) This contention is a desperate attack to usurp ultimate authority from God Himself, and put it into the hands of man. We saw this same struggle played out at the Tower of Babel in Genesis 11, when men sought to become more powerful than God, erroneously trying to make Him irrelevant.

The greatest victory that the humanists believe they can win in order to declare ultimate authority over God is the control over life and death. Holding the final authority over who can live and who must die is their greatest aim– which is why abortion is the battle they will not let go of. Interestingly, we could have predicted that once they believed they'd won the right to kill the babies, the elderly would be their next target, and that's exactly what we saw in the vulnerability of the elderly to the coronavirus.

Man has historically sought to prove that ultimate authority rests in him, not in God. The deception has become the motto, "My body, my choice!" Man has always sought to be God, and the abortion issue has been the primary battleground. There are very evil forces at work, and unfortunately, many women have been sucked into the deception, often through blind naivety.

In this fallen world, there are so many women who have experienced frustration, panic, or even anger finding out they were pregnant, and it's always because of sin– their sin, or someone else's.

Perhaps it was sin through the horrific means by which the child was conceived; maybe it was sin because of being worn down by our fallen world that has been too hard to survive in ourselves, let alone raise a child in; maybe it was sin because of selfish desires and plans that a child would interfere with; perhaps it's fear of the unknown, or fear of previous bad experiences that have turned the joy of the miracle into panic and frustration.

Sometimes I wistfully wonder what childbirth would have been like had Adam and Eve not sinned. I don't have to think about it for long. We know that pain in childbirth was a curse because of Eve's sin (Genesis 3:16). If there had not been sin, there would not have had to be pain, which is a picture of the pain and suffering Jesus would have to endure in redeeming us from our sin, providing the way for us to be born again into true life, into His everlasting Kingdom.

But in cursing Eve, He never took away the miracle of conception and childbirth. Children are not the curse. Giving birth is not the curse. Pain is the curse. Death is the curse.

Children are the redeeming joy of the pain. Children are the reward of painful circumstances, just as we are the reward of Jesus' undeserved suffering.

> Psalm 127:3-5 says, "Behold, children are a heritage from the Lord, the fruit of the womb a reward. Like arrows in the hand of a warrior are the children of one's youth. Blessed is the man who fills his quiver with them."

There are many reasons why women are filled with sadness– or anger, or frustration, or fear– upon realizing that they are expecting a baby. Some of them are understandably angry because conception was a product of rape. Although many Christians consider abortion to be an acceptable– maybe the only acceptable– way to deal with such a heinous crime, it simply is not. Of the three individuals who are involved in this crime, only the father is the criminal. The mother is the devastated victim.

The baby– the most innocent of all– cannot purchase justice by dying a horrific and tortuous execution in an attempt to pay for the sins of an unrepentant criminal father. Jesus gave His life in a torturous death, once for all, that the sins of the repentant might be forgiven, and it's already accomplished. The criminal father must bear the punishment of his own sin, and can only find forgiveness through repentance and faith in Christ– never through the blood sacrifice of the child he conceived. Not one innocent person must die again in order to forgive the sins of someone else.

It is never justice to execute the innocent baby while the unrepentant father goes free. He himself must pay the consequence of his own sin.

Our whole culture needs to stand strongly with the women who have been violated through rape by assuring that the criminals who have violated them are punished and prohibited from repeating their heinous acts. Unfortunately, aborting the baby who was conceived by rape interferes with the process of justice because it destroys the evidence of the crime, and thereby enables the criminal to continue his horrific violations. He gets away totally without consequence– free to do it again and again– while the abortion destroys the very evidence that could have convicted him.

> "The soul who sins shall die. The son shall not suffer for the iniquity of the father, nor the father suffer for the iniquity of the son..." (Ezekiel 18:20).

We must never make light of the horrific circumstance of rape. There is no way in the universe that it can be anything less than gross violation and the heinous abuse that it is.

We must also never make light of the horrific circumstance of Jesus' crucifixion– of the pain, of the gross injustice of those who spat on Him, humiliated Him, beat Him, bloodied His body. Ripping His clothes off, they hung Him naked and shameful by nails in His wrists and feet. When He was thirsty, they scornfully gave Him sour wine, and finally they pierced His side with a spear.

There was not one element of this humiliation and afflicted pain that He deserved. He is the only man who was ever completely innocent, and yet He bore it so that He could bring the repentant soul into life everlasting.

Just as our own life in the Kingdom of Heaven is the redeeming joy of Christ's suffering, so also the child who was conceived in grossly sinful, painful circumstances is the redeeming joy of the mother's suffering.

Multiple stories are cropping up all over the internet telling of individuals who were conceived by rape, or of mothers who chose to keep the children they conceived from rape. Without exception, they are all saying the very same thing in words that express: "Stop saying my life is not worth living! Stop saying my life has no value because of how I was conceived! Stop saying I should have died!"

There is not a single case that I know of where the person who was conceived in rape would agree that it would have been justifiable to have had their own life executed before they were born.

Like Louis Armstrong, every individual has the right to live a fruitful and productive life, regardless of the circumstances in which they were conceived or born. The individuals who were conceived by rape– or by accident, or at an inconvenient time, or through dire suffering– have the same value, and the same right to life in the sight of God and man as those who were conceived in ideal circumstances.

There's no way around it: the world is filled with suffering and it will never be any other way until God recreates it without sin. Suffering is the character of life on this present earth– and yet suffering can either produce death, or life. By identifying with Christ in His suffering, we become more like Him, and life has the final word. Life has the final victory.

Philippians 3:8-10 is one of the richest passages in the Bible. In it, Paul who suffered a great deal and died a martyr's death wrote so incredibly that,

> "I count everything as loss because of the surpassing worth of knowing Christ Jesus my Lord. For his sake I have suffered the loss of all things and count them as rubbish, in order that I may gain Christ and be found in him ...
>
> "...that I may know him and the power of his resurrection, and may share in his sufferings, becoming like him in his death..."

There are women who suffer a great deal in this life, and I believe that as they identify with Christ in His suffering, they will be rewarded– some as martyrs– in the next. It's in knowing the full spectrum of who God is– knowing not only the power of His resurrection life, but also knowing the fellowship of His suffering– that we will be formed into His image as we are found in Him.

There are currently multitudes of women who have suffered through horrific circumstances that resulted in conception, who have been deceived into believing that aborting their babies will give them peace. But it won't and it doesn't. A dead baby cannot take away the memories or the repercussions of their suffering. Only Jesus can do that because He knows the pain of abuse like no one else.

There are multitudes of women who have reacted wrongly by aborting their babies as they were driven by their own fears, humiliations, or by selfish desires. And yet all of these can find forgiveness in Christ Jesus.

The Gospel is always a message of hope. Sin, no matter how deep, can be forgiven through repentance and faith in the atoning work of Christ. The great hope and amazing truth of the Gospel is this completion of the verse from Ezekiel mentioned above:

> "But if a wicked person turns away from all his sins that he has committed and keeps all my statues and does what is just and right, he shall surely live; he shall not die," (Ezekiel 18:21).

And that's exactly the message of the Kingdom we now belong to– that Jesus carried our sins and griefs upon Himself, making the way for us to find forgiveness through His suffering that we might be born into His resurrection life.

Don't be surprised that there is sin and suffering in this world– but be amazed and incredibly grateful that there is forgiveness, full and certain. Only God Himself can redeem our sin and create something so beautiful out of the ashes of our ruins.

Anyone who has seen the birth of a baby can understand that.

Anyone who believes, finds life in Him.

CHAPTER 17
Heaven

After my Dad passed away, my sister sat at her desk on a dark, sleepless night staring out the window at the full moon high up in the starry sky– so peaceful, so calm, so beautiful. "Where is heaven?" she wondered. "Where is Dad right now?"

Where is heaven?

How close is it?

The Bible tells of many times when mortal man was given a glimpse of heaven. In 2 Kings 2:11, Elisha watched as a vehicle of some kind appeared and whisked Elijah into a deeper dimension, into heaven, separating the two of them.

I frequently wonder what kind of vehicle it was. Elisha could only describe what he saw in terms that he understood at the time within the context of his culture– some kind of flaming horse and fiery chariot. But in heaven, technology as we know it is so much beyond the primitive ideas that we think are so advanced here right now. Maybe the vehicle was actually what we'd describe now as something closer to the Millennium Falcon in the Star Wars movies.

1 Chronicles 21:16 recalls one of many times when David repented after he had sinned, and this time his eyes were opened briefly to see the connection between earth and heaven– the proximity of which apparently was close enough for him to see.

> "And David lifted his eyes and saw the angel of the Lord standing between earth and heaven..."

It was a dimension, not a distance, that David's eyes were opened to see. Heaven was surrounding David, and for a brief moment, his eyes were open to see it through another dimension.

Throughout history, others have been graced with a glimpse of heaven. Genesis 28:12 is the record of when Jacob saw heaven in a dream, where a ladder reached to heaven and angels of God were ascending and descending it.

Paul's eyes were likewise opened to see heaven as recorded in 2 Corinthians 12, but the description of it defied words.

The first chapter of Revelation tells of John being on the Isle of Patmos when his eyes were opened to see heaven.

Every one of these experiences must have been akin to standing on the deck of a ship looking over the endless emptiness and apparent loneliness of the vast ocean, as I have done. Then imagine– as I did– that suddenly the water becomes miraculously transparent enough to reveal the incredible marine world that's teeming with life just under the surface– a world that we are normally blind to; a world that normally our limited humanity prevents us from seeing, though it's so close.

Heaven is not visible to us because it's in a dimension we have not yet experienced. Right now, we are confined to three dimensions of space plus one dimension of time, which severely limits us in our human ability to grasp some things that are even very close to us.

In reality, heaven and earth are close, and far more connected than we can imagine. They are part of each other. Since Adam's sin in the Garden of Eden– that place where heaven and earth are joined, where God's physical presence interacts with man– man's eyes have been blinded to this nearness as God has left His angels to guard the entrance to this deeper dimension.

Thinking of earth as 'heaven's womb' positions the connection in a more realistic way– if we are in Christ, we are surrounded by heaven, and we are participants of heaven's Kingdom even now, though we have not been released into the fulness of it yet. We will not see it until we are physically birthed by way of a new dimension into heaven.

In the whole context of the revision of her book about heaven, Joni Eareckson Tada reminds us of the primary focus of the eternal Kingdom that we are part of even now.

> "Heaven isn't so much a place as it is a Person... If He's there, it's heaven. If He's not, then it's not."[34]

That phrase is far more significant than you think. It's ironic that in our current culture, there are masses of people who reject God, and yet assume they will go to heaven when they

---

[34] Joni Eareckson Tada, *Heaven Your Real Home–From a Higher Perspective*, (Grand Rapids, Michigan, Zondervan, 2018) Preface,16.

die. When their own loved ones die, they confidently assure us that, "They're in a better place." But are they?

Is heaven the place where we will forever be with our friends? Forever with our children? When we think of heaven, do we think of "people"? Or do we immediately think of all the great perks, like no sickness, no sadness, no tears? Maybe it's the beautiful mansion where we will live that immediately comes to mind, or maybe it's just the comfort we find in wanting to go on living.

Undoubtedly, heaven is all these things, plus more. We will know each other in heaven. The Bible tells us that there will be no more sadness, no more tears. And Jesus said that He was going to prepare for us a home. But there will be an infinitely greater attraction that will capture our deepest affection and our sole attention when we're birthed into it. I Thessalonians 4:16, 17 gives us an idea of what the coming resurrection will be when it describes how

> "...the Lord himself will descend from heaven with a cry of command... we will be caught up together to meet the Lord in the clouds, and so we will always be with the Lord."

This, friends, is our singular anticipation–forever with the Lord.

A couple of years ago, I experienced an understanding of what heaven will be like, more than I had previously grasped. My husband and I love to travel and have been to almost 30 countries. And yet in all our travel adventures, the best by far was when we took our children, including daughters-in-law and son-in-law, with us to the tiny, beloved Tuscan hilltop city of Civita di Bagnoregio in Italy. Ever since Dan and I had discovered this amazing place several years before that, I had dreamed of returning some day with our kids.

Civita was built by the Etruscans c.700 B.C. high atop a pinnacle for fortification. This beautiful, ancient stone city is accessible only by a very long pedestrian bridge that ascends constantly upward. From the base of the bridge, looking way up into the majestic medieval city high up at the top of the pinnacle, I couldn't help but think, "This must be what it will be like when the holy city, New Jerusalem, comes down out of heaven from God, prepared as a bride adorned for her husband," (Rev. 21:2). It was absolutely breathtaking.

Together we trudged up the long bridge. As soon as we passed through the dark stone tunnel of the city gate, we emerged into immediate brightness and the stunning ancient world of long, long ago. Our kids all wandered off in different directions, mesmerized by the beauty of the place. My husband headed off to explore the underground tunnels, and I found myself suddenly alone, wandering through the narrow stone streets of this place I loved so well. Alone, and yet I was inexplicably content as I had never known contentment before.

As I wandered all by myself, it occurred to me that I didn't have to be with people in order to so fully enjoy being here. Just knowing that my husband and my kids were all there too, all of them fully enjoying the beauty of being in this fantastic place like I was, was enough.

It was then that it occurred to me that heaven will be like that. Even if I didn't actually see my children in heaven– though I'm confident I will– it will be absolute contentment knowing that they are there too, fully immersed in the brightness, the beauty, the awesome presence of Christ Himself who is heaven. Heaven is not people, though people will be there. Heaven is God.

If we aren't comfortable in the presence of the eternal God right here, now, then we sure won't be comfortable in heaven. Above all else, heaven is primarily the overwhelming, constant presence of God Himself. If He's there, it's heaven. If He's not, then it's not.

It's easier to understand that because we know that the great contentment of the baby upon his birth is being in his mother's arms. That's his primary comfort, his only desire. He undoubtedly has a home, but he's not focused on seeing it when he's born. He likely has siblings and a family, but that's not his primary concern yet. After being in her for nine months as he grew, the sole focus of his affection is his mother– the goal of his arrival into the world. Separated from mother at birth, the child will not survive. In an infinitely greater way, Jesus is the focus of our affection, the highest goal of our arrival in heaven. He is heaven.

Everything we do on this earth– every word, every attitude, every action– is a preparation by way of trials, successes, adversities, triumphs, and failures, for our eternal destiny, just as the baby in utero is being prepared for birth into the world in every aspect of its development.

If we can grasp the idea of how heaven and earth are connected– with earth being merely the womb of heaven– the compelling focus of our lives will become so much more meaningful. Everything we do, everything we participate in will reflect our eternal purpose. All of our thoughts and ideas will be rooted in our Christian faith. Our relationships, our interactions, our educational choices, the way we dress, the way we conduct our businesses, our political ideas, our works of charity will all be consistent with– in fact focused upon– our faith. Nothing– and I mean nothing– is outside of our faith. In fact, Romans 14: 23 reminds us that anything outside of our faith is sin.

Again, C.S.Lewis so perceptively wrote,

> "If you read history, you will find that the Christians who did most for the present world were just those who thought most of the next....It is since Christians have largely ceased to think of the other world that they have become so ineffective in this. Aim at heaven and you will get earth thrown in; aim at earth, and you will get neither." [35]

Our lives are not a dichotomy, departmentalized into categories whereby some things are subject to our faith but others are not. For those of us who live and move and have

---

35 C.S.Lewis, *Mere Christianity,* (San Francisco, Harper Collins Publishers, 1952) 134

our being in Christ, there is no separation between an earthly kingdom and a Heavenly Kingdom. There is no distinction between sacred and secular. Our faith is all-encompassing, completely comprehensive, and it touches every detail of our lives, with no exceptions. There is no detail of our lives that is not subject to our heavenly citizenship.

At the same time, there is not one detail of life on this planet– in the womb of heaven– that God does not exercise His Sovereignty over. He owns it all, He encircles it all. Abraham Kuyper once said,

> "There is not a square inch of the whole domain of human existence over which Christ, who is Sovereign over all, does not cry, 'Mine!'"[36]

God is all-powerful, all-present, all-knowing, and nothing– not one molecule, not one cell– on this earth is outside of His Sovereign control. He surrounds all of it. He encircles it all. He is working out His divine will and His divine purposes, and we know that He will be victorious.

Heaven is what's real. The Kingdom of Heaven surrounds us, consumes us, and captures our affections. This is what we were born for; this is what we are being prepared for even as we participate in its reality right now.

> "If then you have been raised with Christ, seek the things that are above, where Christ is, seated at the

---

[36] Quote from Kuyper's inaugural address at the dedication of the Free University. Found in *Abraham Kuyper: A Centennial Reader*, ed. James D. Bratt (Eerdmans, 1998), 488

right hand of God. Set your minds on things that are above, not on things the are on earth. For you have died, and your life is hidden with Christ in God. When Christ who is your life appears, then you also will appear with him in glory." (Colossians 3:1-4)

CHAPTER 18

How Can We Keep on Living in Heaven?

Heaven is being in the presence of God– being birthed into that new realm of 'The Kingdom of God' where we can actually see Him face to face, just as the newborn baby can finally see his mother and be held in her physical arms. We will live in the actual presence of His full Light, just as the newborn baby emerges into full light.

We also know from the Bible that one day Christ will return to the earth, our spirits will reunite with our bodies, and we will be caught up together to meet Him in triumphant procession. The new heaven and new earth will be joined in a way that we will actually see, and we will live on the re-created earth, yet without sin and sickness.

Truthfully, with the limitations of our present minds, living again on a re-created earth is far easier to understand than the in-between time that many theologians refer to as the 'Intermediate Heaven'– after our time on the current earth is done and we are birthed into heaven, but before the resurrection when we will be joined again with our glorified bodies and live on the re-created earth.

When our physical bodies are left in the grave, we might wonder how it is that we will keep on living in the Intermediate Heaven. What form will we have? How will we continue to exist without these physical bodies we've become so attached to (pun totally intended)?

A short time after the birth of our eleventh grandchild, I sat with my son Justin– the father of the new baby– at their dining room table, as we tried to absorb the bigness of the fresh miracle that had so recently happened.

He speculated, "Imagine if a baby could talk, what he would say to the midwife: 'Wait! Do not cut that umbilical cord! If you cut that cord, I will die. It's attached to the placenta and it's the only way I can get nourishment! It's the only way I can survive. If you cut that cord, I will stop living. Don't cut that cord!'"

And yet the cord is cut, and the placenta– the very life supply of the growing child– is expelled. Done away with! Suddenly a brand new function begins in that tiny body as the lungs inhale oxygen and exhale carbon dioxide, providing the child with a completely new way to sustain him. His lungs had never worked like that before!

Then he hungrily begins to eat with his mouth– a new idea that he has not had to use before– as food is digested in his stomach, and a completely new way of receiving nourishment begins. He's never known these functions before, and in his wildest imagination, he could not have anticipated them. If we had never experienced this in such a common way ourselves, we too would think it was mind-boggling!

When we are born into heaven, by God's design, we will continue to exist and survive in ways we cannot imagine right now. Just as it's completely natural for us to see a baby gulp his first breath of air, or hungrily suck his mother's milk, the new way by which we will continue to exist in heaven will seem perfectly natural to us when it will happen.

In her book about heaven, Joni Eareckson Tada wrote that when she gets there,

> "...I will bear the likeness of Jesus, the man from heaven. Like His, [my body] will be an actual, literal body perfectly suited for earth and heaven."[37]

Somehow, we will interact with Jesus, who is now in heaven in His resurrected, physical, glorified body.

Philippians 3:20, 21 assures us of this when it says,

> "Our citizenship is in heaven, and from it we await a savior, the Lord Jesus Christ, who will transform our lowly body to be like his glorious body, by the power that enables him even to subject all things to himself."

Randy Alcorn, the author of the book Heaven, referred to theologians like Alister McGrath, Hank Hanegraaff, and the medieval theologian Thomas Aquinas who all speculated that since heaven is a place of perfection– without sin, without disease, disabilities, the affects of old age or decay– our new bodies may look similar to what we looked like at about 30 years of age. [38] That's the time when our earthly bodies have reached their closest point of perfection, before they begin to

---

[37] Joni Eareckson Tada, *Heaven, Your Real Home,* (Grand Rapids, Michigan, Zondervan Publishers, 1995, edited 2018) 55
[38] Randy Alcorn, *Heaven,* (Tyndale House Publishers, 2004) 289

decline. It was this point of bodily perfection when Jesus Himself left His life on this earth and went back to the Father in heaven.

Our elderly parents will not be bent over with arthritis or riddled with Alzheimers; the disabled will be whole. Only Jesus Himself will forever bear the physical marks of His suffering in His hands and feet as the perpetual testament of His sacrifice to bring us there.

For a newborn baby to transition from being sustained via the umbilical cord to using lungs that take in oxygen and breathe out carbon dioxide is a very natural process. It seems so obvious. Likewise, when we see God's design for us in heaven, it will seem so "right," that we will probably respond, as C.S. Lewis had said to his friend Sheldon Vanauken that we would. "Why, of course! Of course it's like this. How else could it have possibly been." [39]

Sometimes I honestly wonder if I am the only person on the planet who has felt some confusion about what heaven will be like according to the descriptions of it from the Bible. We speculate about creatures with four wings and four faces – one like a lion, one like an ox, one like an eagle, one like a human. We try to imagine living creatures full of eyes in front and behind, or streets of gold, or city gates of giant pearls. Really?

---

[39] Sheldon Vanauken, *A Severe Mercy,* (New York, NY, Harper Collins Publishers, 1977) 125

But again, imagine if we could somehow tell the little child in utero what's ahead of him in the world into which he will be born. Blazing red skies at sunset; creatures with four legs and a tail called dogs and cats, and even growling big ones like lions; or strange and ugly ones like the rhinoceros or the porcupine or the sloth, or scorpions or toads; lightning flashing across the sky; cars and buses and airplanes... Would the child have reservations about what's ahead?

When the child is born, none of this matters when he is placed into the physical arms of his mother. Is she what he had always imagined? It doesn't matter. After being in her for nine months, his mother is the sole comfort, the ultimate happiness of his birth into the world. Everything else is peripheral, and all of it becomes normal– even appreciated– as time goes on.

After a baby has left the dark confines of the womb and is born into the light, aromas, space, color, beauty of the earth, placed into the warm physical embrace of his mother, no child would choose instead to return to the dark, crowded confines of the womb. None. Not one. It's impossible.

Once we are born into heaven, there will be absolutely no desire to return to the dark confines of earth when compared to the wonder, the beauty, the color, the indescribable peace and contentment of being embraced in the physical arms of Jesus. What ecstasy. What peace. What total and complete contentment.

As a very young girl, I listened, fascinated, as a speaker at a summer camp compared entering heaven to walking from one room filled with noisy, relentless machinery into another room of total and absolute quiet. It's impossible to even comprehend the degree of peace.

It would be absolutely impossible for us to want to return to the limited, dark confines of earth, to the pressure and stresses laid upon us, to the heavy weight of the sin that saturates the present world, any more than a baby would prefer to return to the darkness and confinement of the womb.

One of my grandkids had a troubling dream that I had died. Consequently, his mother brought him to me so that he could have he assurance that I was, in fact, still here. I took his little face in my hands and said, "One day, sweetheart, it's going to happen. Some day, you'll find out that I really have died. When you hear it, I know that you'll be sad– but I want you to know that when that happens, I will be very, very happy, and I want you to be happy with me. Heaven is my home, and when I am in the arms of Jesus, I will be happier than ever before! My life will be more real than ever before. My life will only be starting.That's what dying is going to be."

At that moment when we enter heaven, in a very real way, our lives will only have just begun. Our time on earth– this time of preparation in the womb of heaven– is not our truest reality; it is not our final home; it is not our ultimate destination, nor is it the fulfillment of our gifts, talents, joys, or happiness. What we know here, now, is just the mirage that Lewis wrote about. It's merely the parable that Jesus taught. It's only seeing through a glass darkly, as I Corinthians 13:12 expresses.

We cannot yet know what form our bodies will have when we arrive in the Intermediate Heaven, but we do know that the reality we will experience will be far greater than anything we can possibly know on this earth. We will truly be "home."

CHAPTER 19

The Kingdom We Were Created For

When I was a child, my Dad told a story about a poor Ukrainian man in the Old Country riding down a lonely, dusty road in his horse-drawn wagon when he noticed a tired traveler lumbering laboriously down the dirty road. The man stopped his wagon to pick up the weary traveler.

The traveler– a Christian– was grateful for the kindness and saw this as a good opportunity to extend even greater kindness by sharing the gospel. So after a little bit of awkward silence, he turned abruptly and introduced his well-intended idea by asking, "Are you ready to die?"

The man with the wagon immediately assumed he was being robbed, so with lightning speed, he beat the traveler, pushed him out of the wagon and left him wounded by the roadside. The poor, beaten traveler limped his way home, and when he got there he bragged to his family that he had suffered for the sake of the gospel.

What strange ideas we Christians likewise have sometimes when we want to share the good news of the Kingdom of Heaven– though hopefully not as carelessly as this traveler did. The gospel is good news: we can have the sure promise of our inheritance in the Kingdom of Heaven.

But when does that promise begin? When we are born again, is the promise of the Kingdom of God for our future in heaven? Or is the reality of the Kingdom of God on earth, here, now?

And the answer is, "Yes!"

Far too often, our minds have forced heaven and earth into an erroneous separation– totally disconnected from each other. On the one hand, there are those of us whose only goal in life is to get to heaven. I grew up in the church where, much like the traveler in the story above, there were children's evangelists who asked the only question that seemed to matter to them, "Do you want to go to heaven when you die?" To them, like it was for the confused traveler, life is merely a waiting room for marking time until we get to our eternal bliss.

On the other hand, even now there are many individuals who have no interest at all in the hereafter– whether Christian or not. Heaven to them is some sort of wispy non-physical world, a nebulous, old-fashioned ghostly setting where we will float around as though in a dream; a place where everything stops– our gifts and talents, our projects, our activities, our desires, our interests– in order to enter a state of everlasting drifting.

Yet both of these ideas are so far from the magnificent reality of the Kingdom of Heaven that we are purposeful, active participants in now, and yet will know in its fulness when we are born into heaven.

In truth, earth and heaven are much more connected than we can even imagine, and together they comprise the very real Kingdom of God– where God Himself through Christ Jesus is the center– to which we have been called to actively participate in. As wonderful as our life in the Kingdom of God is right now, Ephesians 1:13 and 14 reminds us that this is merely the downpayment of our full inheritance.

Our time here on earth is important! This Kingdom is marked with fruitfulness, and we are actively being prepared for its fulness ahead. What we do now [on earth] is shaping us for the full reality of the Kingdom [in heaven] that we belong to.

Psalm 1 urges us toward this reality when it contrasts those in the Kingdom of God with those who are outside of it:

> "The man [whose delight is in the law of the Lord] is like a tree planted by streams of water, that yields its fruit in its season and its leaf does not wither. The wicked are no so, but are like chaff that the wind drives away... The Lord knows the way of the righteous, but the way of the wicked will perish."

The Kingdom of God is characterized by fruitfulness, whereas the Kingdom of darkness is characterized by barrenness- like dry, fruitless chaff blown by the wind. The dry chaff is evident in the relentless determination of our current culture to kill the babies– the next generation– and to distort marriage itself in such a way that the ultimate satisfaction is self-satisfaction. Instead of creating life, it defies it, scoffs at it– the ultimate demonstration of selfishness.

In his commentary of Romans and Galatians, R.J. Rushdoony quoted Steward Brand, creator of The Whole Earth Catalogue [40] boasting about his hope for disaster when he wrote,

> "We have wished, we ecofreaks, for a disaster, or for a dramatic social change to come and bomb us into the Stone Age, where we might live like Indians in our valley, with our localism, our Appropriate Technology, our gardens and our homemade religion, guilt-free at last."[41]

The kingdom of this world craves darkness and barrenness in their futile attempt to satisfy the guilt that all men are born with– guilt that can only be satisfied through faith in Christ who paid the ransom for our sin. Only then can we enter the guilt-free Kingdom of His Son, characterized – thanks be to God– by life and fruitfulness.

In Matthew 25:14-30, Jesus had some very significant things to say about the Kingdom of God when He told His disciples a parable of the talents. In it, the Master gave one of his servants five talents. To a second servant, he gave two talents, and to a third servant he gave one talent.

A talent is a unit of weight of approximately 80 lbs (or 36 kg.) When used as money, it referred specifically to that weight in silver. One talent was equal to 6,000 denarii, the common currency. To help us understand the value, remember that one

---

[40] R.J.Rushdoony, *Commentary of Romans and Galatians* (Wallecito, CA, Ross House Publishing, 1997) 43

[41] Herbert I. London, *Why Are They Lying to Our Children*, Stein and Day Publishers, 1984) 151

denarius was the usual payment for a day's labor. Recall Jesus' parable of paying the laborers each a denarius in Matthew 20, even though they began work at different times.

Understanding the great value of these talents, the meaning of this parable is much more significant. The first servant invested his five talents, and got a return of five more; the second servant likewise invested, and doubled the value. But the third servant, afraid of the Master, dug a hole and buried it so he wouldn't lose it. As we know, the Master was pleased with the two who had invested, but angry with the one who had hidden his talents.

This parable is a picture of the Kingdom of God, characterized by fruitfulness and increase. Created by God for His glory, we are all given individual responsibility to be good stewards of our gifts and talents, our time and money. While we're on earth– in the womb of heaven– we are called to develop and increase those gifts and talents. The wise servants who invested their money were examples of transformation, of growth, of fruitfulness, of life.

The foolish servant who refused to make use of what he'd been given, but buried it in fear showed no signs of life in the Kingdom. There was no transformation. There was no fruit. What a sad commentary.

Jesus spent his teaching years communicating what the Kingdom of Heaven was like by teaching parables. Life and fruitfulness characterized so many of these, like the parable of the farmer sowing seeds in Luke 8:9-15, which He summed up saying, "Bear fruit with patience."

"Each tree is known by its own fruit," He said in Luke 6:44, encouraging the examination of the fruit of one's life.

When He taught the parable of the barren fig tree in Luke 13:6-9, He said,

> "If it should bear fruit next year, well and good; but if not, you can cut it down."

In Luke 13:14-19 He said that the Kingdom of God was like mustard seed that was sown in a farmer's garden that grew and increased, and in verse 20, He said it was like leaven that increased.

Life and fruitfulness mark the character of the Kingdom of Heaven. We were created by God to be fruitful, for the sake of His glory, not ours. Jesus said in John 15:16:

> "You did not choose me, but I chose you and appointed you that you should go and bear fruit, and that your fruit should abide..."

With our eyes fixed on Jesus Christ and His glory– the center of the Kingdom– consider what this "fruit" looks like.

The first and primary fruit that comes from new birth is **repentance**. John the Baptist was the forerunner of Jesus who prepared the way for His coming by preaching relentlessly about the fruit of repentance. He was ruthless in his criticism of the Pharisees and Sadducees who arrogantly assumed that by their own works they were made holy. They personified *self*-righteousness yet had no evidence of the fruit of the Righteousness imputed only from God, characterized first and foremost by repentance. The fruit of the Righteousness of God is completely different than the fruit of self-righteousness.

It's only when we truly see our own worthlessness, confess our own sin, and acknowledge our own humility, that we are properly prepared to be used by God for *His* glory. John showed us the way in his deep and heartfelt prayer written in John 3:30 that he himself would decrease so that Christ would increase, for the sake of God's glory and not man's. It's in this humility that God can finally make us fruitful as we abide in Him.

God has given us the privilege of being participants in His Story, where He is the star of the show. No one's attention ought to focus on any of the supporting actors; all of them point to the main focus, the sole Hero of the story. As members of an orchestra whose individual parts are done well, together we must draw the attention away from individual musicians into the ultimate story of the musical masterpiece. That's when God can increase our gifts and talents for His glory. That's what we are being formed and prepared for.

"Bear fruit worthy of repentance..." John warned the Pharisees in John 3:7-10.

> "Every tree that does not bear fruit is cut down and thrown into the fire!"

Repentance is the sorrow expressed for having offended God, and we have all offended God. But more than that, repentance involves change– a change of heart and mind. There is no life in Christ without the fruit of repentance.

What is the fruit of repentance, the evidence of the work of the Holy Spirit in our lives?

"**The fruit of the Spirit** is love, joy, peace, patience, kindness, goodness, faithfulness, gentleness, self-control; against such things there is no law," Galatians 5:22-23 tells us as it clearly defines the fruit that is evident in those who are in Christ Jesus.

But be on guard! The current culture, we must note, has become adept at imposing their anti-godly agenda by way of manipulating the very definitions of these godly characteristics, the true fruit of the Holy Spirit.

"Love" is misrepresented by lust in order to force everyone into widespread acceptance of every kind of sexual perversion. "Joy" has been replaced with "whatever makes you happy," creating a deeply self-centered culture that refuses to take responsibility for harmful actions. The word "peace" has been used as a tool of manipulation to force us into cooperation with an anti-God agenda. "Kindness" is widely misused as a means of forcing the culture to embrace perversion and heartily accept every humanistic, anti-Christian behavior. "Goodness" itself is redefined as a characteristic of those who accept perversion.

Every form of sin is a perversion of the good that God has blessed us with. Consequently, the manipulation of this present devious culture will twist the very character of the fruit of the Kingdom of Light in order to deceive and manipulate us into compliance with the kingdom of darkness. We must recognize it, and refuse it, standing firm in God's truth.

Just as Romans 12:9,10 provides depth and understanding of the true character of "love"–

> "Let love be genuine. Abhor what is evil; hold fast to what is good. Love one another with brotherly affection. Outdo one another in showing honor,"

– so must every fruit of the Spirit also be defined and measured according to the Bible.

If we truly abide in Him, we will not have to strive to bear the fruit of His Kingdom. Like the baby in utero, our time on earth– in the womb of heaven– is a time of preparation for life in the Kingdom that we are already part of, but have not yet entered into the eternal fulfillment of.

Just prior to Jesus' telling the parable of the talents, He had said, "The Kingdom of Heaven is like..." and went on to tell the parable of the ten virgins. Five were wise, and kept their lamps filled with oil, while the other five were foolish, and weren't as vigilant. Consequently, when the bridegroom came, they were not prepared– and they missed him. The Kingdom of God is marked by preparedness.

Our time on earth is a time of preparation– just as it is for a baby in utero. It's the time of growing, maturing, developing skills and talents, applying our faith to all of life, understanding what it is that we believe, becoming equipped to enter the fullness of His everlasting Kingdom where all of our development will have meaning and purpose.

CHAPTER 20
Vitally Alive in the Womb of Heaven

In the early days of this current millennium, my husband and I were actively involved with a Christian political party, joining with many others in applying the principles of God's Word to the civil sphere. Understandably, there had been many battles in this work, and there were many times that we were deeply discouraged, wondering if there was any fruit we could see.

At a point of discouragement and weariness, I had asked someone to pray for Dan in this ministry, as it was sometimes terribly hard. I was truly stunned at her reply. "Ministry?" she scoffed. "This isn't 'ministry'! It's politics!"

That response floored me. Was all this hard work really 'just politics,' I wondered? Were there actually areas of life, like this one, where our faith in God was inappropriate?

Reeling from the response, it occurred to me that sadly, there really is a vast majority of professing evangelical Christians who are living in the dichotomy that Nancy Pearcey wrote about in her book Total Truth– a dichotomy whereby faith in God applies to some areas, but not others. And yet, as she wrote in her Introduction, there is no question that,

> "The most effective work [in this world]... is done by ordinary Christians fulfilling God's calling to reform culture within their local spheres of influence– their

> families, churches, schools, neighborhoods, workplaces, professional organizations, and civic institutions." [42]

We cannot even imagine the great impact Christians would make if we truly lived out our faith in every area of life, with no exceptions, beginning right where we are.

This truth became vividly alive to me in merely a moment's time when I sat listening to my husband once, long ago, speaking to a large audience at a meeting for the Christian political party we were involved with at the time. As he spoke, in my mind's eye, it seemed like I was suddenly looking through a window, and as I peered through it from this side, the view on the other side, though limited, was remarkably clear and bright, with more color and acute precision than anything I'd ever seen before.

It was such a small thought and the clarity of it lasted for only a few seconds; but strangely, it energized me to realize that the work we do while we're here on earth is all part of something far bigger, brighter, clearer, far more grand and lasting than we can imagine. It extends far beyond what we know here, now. We don't yet see with clarity; our vision of God's full plan is still foggy to us. And yet we have to understand that what we are doing is not just for now, but for eternity.

---

[42] Nancy Pearcey, *Total Truth*, (Wheaton, Illinois, Crossway Publishers, 2004),19

There is no separation between what's "sacred" and what's "secular." Everything we do while we're here on earth– in the womb of heaven– is connected to the far greater reality of the Kingdom of Heaven to which we belong, and the fullness of which we will someday be physically born into. R.J. Rushdoony wrote,

> "Good works do not save us, but if good works are separated from salvation, we have neither salvation nor good works. The just are saved by faith, and they live and work by faith." [43]

What we do now– in the womb of heaven– is vital in our preparation for the eternal.

An earlier chapter made reference to 'the call of God on your life' as sometimes being a call to suffer. Most often, though, we fail to recognize the call of God on our lives because it comes wrapped in what's so "ordinary"- in the normal tasks of predictable life. And yet we fail to comprehend the immeasurable impact that we have in faithfully fulfilling God's call for us. We're too blinded by the faithful "ordinary," too easily distracted by expecting something spectacular.

The call of God on my own mother's life was the humble yet powerful gift of hospitality, though I don't think she ever recognized the great impact it had. As a child, I grew up with people constantly in our home, around our dinner table, and in our living room talking. Through all those years, I

---

[43] R.J.Rushdoony, *Commentary on Romans and Galatians*, (Vallecito, CA, Ross House Books Publishing, 1997) 87

remember my mother constantly hustling about in the kitchen, keeping the coffee hot, serving others, making meals, pumping out cookies, making beds and squeezing guests into our small home so that everybody who entered felt welcomed.

There were times when she wistfully commented about her regret that she hadn't "become something"- a professional seamstress, a teacher, a writer... Yet at her memorial service, I was stunned at the scores and scores of people who crowded into the chapel to honor her memory. She herself would have been completely astonished at the number of those who came– all of whom had been recipients of her hospitality in some form over those many years. We will never know the full impact of how so many of these were ministered to, refreshed, encouraged, strengthened by her hospitality. Her calling was far more significant than she herself had ever recognized because it was too easy for her, too "ordinary."

And yet, it's in the normal, ordinary aspects of life that we fulfill God's greatest commands.

What have you been given in this life? It matters! To a mother caring for her children– raising them to be faithful, active members of the Kingdom to which we belong– this is what God has given her to do. The powerful affect of this work must never be underestimated.

We must be careful not to dismiss the great task of a mother's calling because it seems so ordinary. Training her children to embrace and apply a comprehensive Christian worldview that will defeat the chaos of the enemy is the greatest assignment a woman will ever be given on this earth. The culture may seem dark around us, and the war is real. But Jeremiah 29:4-7 gives us the battle plan for our strategy: "Multiply there, and do not decrease!"

We must increase the biblical thinkers who can astound the chaos of this present world with sound, biblical reasoning and a firm biblical worldview that will defeat every attack of the evil enemies of God. This is the call of God on the Christian mother, most powerfully delineated on a monument to the Pilgrim mothers in Plymouth, Massachusetts:

> "They brought up their families in sturdy virtue and a living faith in God, without which nations perish."

In 1859 Rev. S. Phillips wrote,

> "The Christian home...forms the citizen, lays the foundation for civil and political character, prepares the social element and taste, and determines our national prosperity or adversity. We owe to the family, therefore, what we are as a nation as well as [what we are as] individuals."[44]

Too often, we feel like we can "relax" when we're at home with our family. Tongues slip easily, slander and gossip creep into conversations, and we slide carelessly into watching questionable or edgy shows on tv. And yet the home is the very place where the authenticity of our faith is tested, and where it has the greatest impact. The reality of what we believe is demonstrated first and foremost in the home before

---

[44] S. Phillips in Rosalie Slater's *Teaching and Learning America's Christian History: The Principle Approach* (San Francisco, CA, 1965)

it is shown anywhere else. It's in the home that our faith has the greatest affect. Psalm 101: 2,3 says,

> "I will walk with integrity of heart within my house; I will not set before my eyes anything that is worthless..."

Faith is most powerfully applied in the home, and as mothers, we must be equipped, fruitful, and prepared in it.

If you are in business, then this is what God has given you as a faithful steward, to the glory of God and the advancement of His Kingdom on the earth. Does your character reflect Christ as you interact with others in your business transactions? Do the practices and actions you demonstrate in your business consistently follow the principles and commands of our Christian faith? Do you pray for those you work with? Do you live according to the Law of God, the truth and principles of His Kingdom revealed to us in the Bible as you go through your day to day actions and responsibilities?

If you are a teacher, or doctor, or musician, or engineer, or designer, you are commanded to live out the Kingdom of Heaven in your work, doing everything as unto the Lord, because it is indeed preparation for your eternal destiny, and it advances the Kingdom of Heaven on the earth. There is not one single area of a Christian's life that is not subject to the faith.

Here in the world, obviously, we see everything in a very limited way. 1 Corinthians 13:12 reminds us,

> "Now we see in a mirror dimly, but then face to face. Now I know in part; then, I shall know fully, even as as have been fully known."

When we are born into heaven itself, we will see it all very clearly.

We were created for infinitely more than what we see right now. We were created, and are in the current process of being formed and prepared for the Kingdom of Heaven that we belong to now, but will know in its fullness later. Our gifts and talents won't suddenly stop in heaven; they will continue with more clarity and perfection, for the glory of God and the fulfillment of His Kingdom. We will all be part of the full expression of God's perfect design and purpose, and no man will receive glory: the glory will truly all be God's as His glorious presence physically dwells among us.

These frail, limited minds we have continually fight against the stubborn persistence of time as it keeps pushing us forward. Right now, we can only see time from a linear perspective; we can't yet see it "end-on" as God does, as we will one day. We think we're going to go on living as we are right now. We try to deny the wrinkles, the greying hair, the declining health– clear evidences that time is pushing us relentlessly onward (I speak from abundant experience.)

We can fruitlessly try to stop it, or at least slow down the process; but life as we know it isn't going to stay the same. We can't stop time. There are moments when we angrily think of time as our enemy– but it isn't.

Time is our friend, pushing us ever closer to the full revelation of what we were created for. R.J.Rushdoony wrote,

> "Time is not for us a dreary round leading only unto death. Despite its ugly discoloration by sin, it is a glorious process of redemption. Time is God's feast-time for men. The six days have their griefs and troubles, but on the seventh we declare our faith and celebrate life and victory." [45]

Psalm 90:10 grabs us by the shoulders, looks us in the eye, and reminds us that,

> "The years of our life are seventy, or even by reason of strength eighty... they are soon gone, and we fly away..."

But that's not a sad thought! It's an exciting, challenging one! It challenges us in our faith toward fruitfulness and preparation as we consider the shortness of our time on earth, and the magnificent greatness of what's ahead for us. A baby's time in the womb is nine short months. Our time in the womb of heaven is a short seventy or perhaps eighty years.

Therefore, "teach us to number our days, that we may get a heart of wisdom," Psalm 90 goes on to say in verse 12. Understanding that we are family members born into the Kingdom of Heaven is our greatest joy, our incomprehensible delight. And yet, it's only the preparation– the dress rehearsal– for what's ahead.

---

[45] R.J.Rushdoony, *Exodus,* (Vallecito, CA, Ross House Books, 2004) 258

That's why I love the last page of the last book of the Chronicles of Narnia. After the children–Peter, Edmond, and Lucy as well as their parents– had died in a train wreck in England, Lewis wrote,

> "For them it was only the beginning of the real story. All their life in this world and all their adventures in Narnia had only been the cover and the title page. Now at last they were beginning Chapter One of the Great Story, which no one on earth has read, which goes on forever, in which every chapter is better than the one before." [46]

Time as we know it is our preparation here in the womb of heaven. The fullness of life– our full inheritance in the Kingdom of Heaven– is coming. And when we are born into it, it will finally be "the beginning."

If that tiny baby could only understand the magnificent life that is waiting as he is born into the world! We the sons of God are exactly like that child in utero. As children of the living God, we must gratefully and enthusiastically embrace the life we have right now. Let's fully embrace and enjoy this time of growing, being formed, shaped, equipped– and at the same time, understand that this is just the cover and the title page. The real story has not even begun yet. We're part of something much bigger. We're part of the vast and wonderful Kingdom of Heaven.

---

[46] C.S.Lewis, *The Last Battle,* (New York, McMillian Publishing Company, 1956) 184

If Christians could only understand the fullness of life that is ours– both now and after– in the Kingdom of Heaven! Be content, be excited, be encouraged, be grateful knowing that you are part of something so much greater than what you know right now.

> "There is a place called 'heaven,'" J.R.R.Tolkien wrote, "where the good here unfinished is completed; and where the stories unwritten, and the hopes unfulfilled, are continued. We may laugh together yet." [47]

That's the incomprehensible Kingdom of Heaven that is ours. We are completely immersed in it right now- and yet we have not entered the fulness of what is ahead for us. That's the true reality of what we've been born into as we find our life in Christ; as we live, and move, and have our being in Him.

---

[47] J.R.R.Tolkien, *The Letters of J.R.R. Tolkien*, (ed. Houghton Mifflin Harcourt, 2014)

Made in the USA
Monee, IL
10 June 2021